THE
ATLAS OF
PEOPLE & PLACES

Philip Steele

Copper Beech Books
Brookfield, Connecticut

Produced by
Aladdin Books Ltd
28 Percy Street
London WIT 2BZ

ISBN 0-7613-2719-3 (s&l)
ISBN 0-7613-1632-9 (pbk.)

*First published in the United States
in 2002 by*
Copper Beech Books,
an imprint of
The Millbrook Press
2 Old New Milford Road
Brookfield, Connecticut 06804

Project Management
SGA design & illustration agency
Hadleigh
Suffolk IP7 5AP

Project Manager
Philippa Jackaman (SGA)

Designer
Phil Kay

Editorial Team
Sarah Eason
Jane Parker
Steve Parker

Picture Researcher
Brian Hunter Smart

Illustrators
Carol Daniel
Stephen Sweet

Printed in Belgium
All rights reserved

Cataloging-in-Publication data is
on file at the Library of Congress.

The author, Philip Steele, is a well
known writer of non-fiction for
children. His subjects include the
natural world, peoples and cultures,
history, and social issues.

CONTENTS

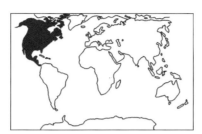
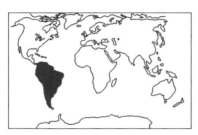
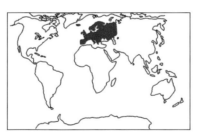
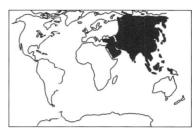

INTRODUCTION

This atlas is about our world and the people who live in it. Have you ever wondered how our planet supports human life? How we make use of natural resources, such as minerals and plants? How life varies from one country to another? Why more and more people live in big cities, and how human activities affect the environment? These are important questions that influence the future of us all.

The planet Earth is huge. It has a surface area of about 197,000,000 sq mi (510,000,000 sq km), of which nearly 30 percent is dry land. The planet has life-giving air and water, supporting a wide range of plants and creatures. About ten percent of dry land can be used to grow crops, 20 percent can be grazed by animals, and about 27 percent is forested. In these types of environment, humans have thrived for many thousands of years. The number of people in the world today has reached about 6.14 billion. By the year 2050 it may have soared to 9.04 billion. Parts of our planet are becoming overcrowded and people need land, minerals such as oil, and ever-increasing amounts of food and water. These needs greatly affect the natural world. Humans clear forests, drain wetlands, and pollute rivers, oceans, the soil, and the air. It is predicted that such interference will change the global climate. In many ways, the future is very uncertain.

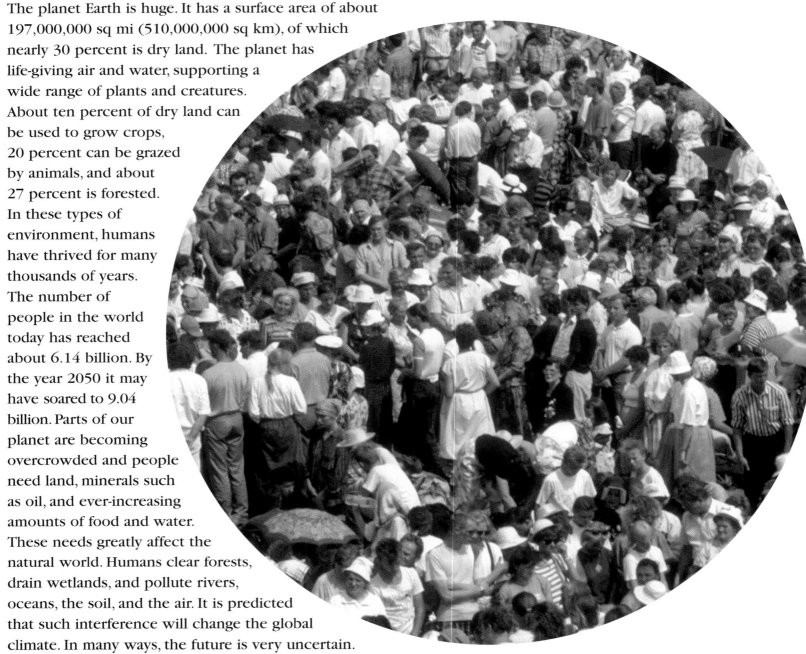

Places to live

Through the ages, people have settled where the climate is mild, where food and fresh water are available, and where land can be farmed. Transportation is also important, by land, sea, or river. About ten percent of the planet is icebound and 20 percent of dry land is desert—in these very harsh conditions, few people can survive.

The first people

All living things on Earth have evolved (developed and changed) over millions of years, as they became suited or adapted to the constantly changing environment. All creatures are related. Humans are most closely related to apes. The earliest remains of humanlike creatures are from Africa. One was a female, found in 1974 in Ethiopia. She was nicknamed "Lucy." Her fossilized bones are more than 3 million years old and show that she was about 3 ft 4 in (1 m) tall and walked upright.

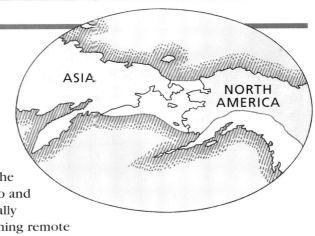

On the move

From 1 million years ago, groups of ancient humans began to develop separately in Africa, Asia, and Europe. Modern humans had probably appeared in Africa by 100,000 years ago. They have been on the move ever since, spreading into and settling new lands, and eventually exploring the oceans and reaching remote islands. Prehistoric hunters from Southeast Asia populated Australia, probably more than 40,000 years ago. North Asian hunters crossed into North America at a time when the two continents were joined by a land bridge. These great historical movements of people into new lands were called migrations.

World population increase

8000 B.C.	6 million
1 A.D.	255 million
1250	416 million
1700	679 million
1800	954 million
1900	1.6 billion
2001	6.14 billion

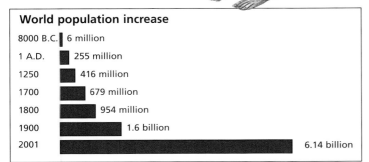

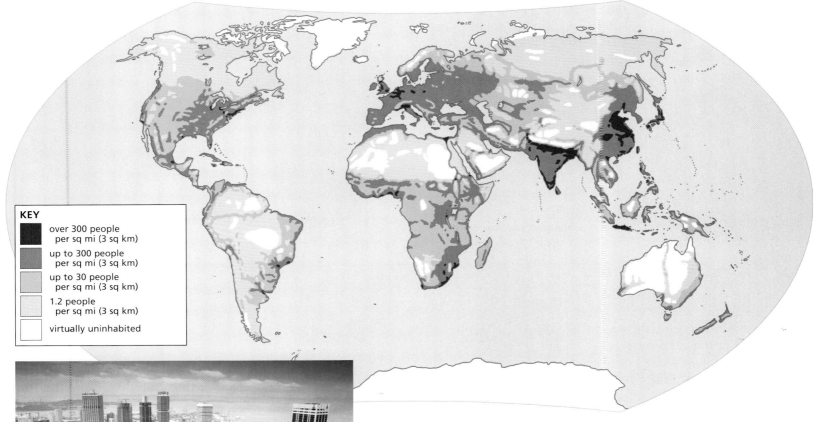

KEY

- over 300 people per sq mi (3 sq km)
- up to 300 people per sq mi (3 sq km)
- up to 30 people per sq mi (3 sq km)
- 1.2 people per sq mi (3 sq km)
- virtually uninhabited

City life

Once people had learned to farm, about 12,000 years ago, they no longer had to hunt for their food. They could settle in one place, trade, and build towns. Over the ages, towns grew into big cities as more and more people arrived from the countryside. Today's cities are enormous and often crowded. In Japan, about 35 million people live in the region around Tokyo, Yokohama, and Kawasaki. Where space is limited, people build upward, creating landscapes of skyscrapers, as in Singapore.

MANY PEOPLES

Modern travel and communications have helped to bring the peoples of the world in touch with one another. Today, human lives everywhere are shaped by the same political events, by the same trading and commerce, and by the same sports and entertainment. With satellite television, we can now view events on the other side of the world—even as they happen! In many other respects, however, different peoples still lead very different lives. Some are very poor, others are very rich. Some are country dwellers, while others live in cities.

People who share a common ancestry, language, and customs are often described as an "ethnic group." Some countries encompass many different ethnic groups, while others have just one. The culture of a group (their way of life) can also vary in many ways, from the preparation of food to the choice of clothes and hairstyles.

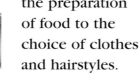

Many Dutch people have pale, pink skin, blond (fair) hair, and blue eyes.

Straight black hair, narrow eyes, and a yellowish complexion are features of most Chinese people.

The human code

Each person contains a chemical substance called DNA, which has a twisted, corkscrew shape. DNA forms genes—instructions that determine the body's features. Genes pass from one generation to the next, which is why children look like their parents. DNA analysis shows that each of us is a unique individual, but the differences between the peoples on Earth are tiny. We are all part of one large family.

Australian Aboriginal people often have broad faces, dark skin, and wavy black hair.

Malinke people of West Africa have brown skin and curly black hair.

Our shared experiences

This mother and child are San. The San people live around the Kalahari Desert in Southern Africa. Their traditional way of life is to hunt animals and gather plants for food. This may seem very different from the lifestyle of a mother and baby in North America, Asia, or Europe. However, all these people share the same basic human experiences. They are all born, they grow up, and they learn how to speak and communicate and how to survive and care for others. They share the same emotions, such as hope, disappointment, love, and anger.

How we look

Over the ages, human beings have adapted to regional conditions and differing ways of life. People developed various bodily features, such as the pigments (coloring) of their skin and hair, depending on where in the world they lived. Siberian people probably developed narrow eyes as a protection against extreme cold and the dazzling white color of snowfields. In hot countries, people developed brown or black skin as a protection against the sun's dangerous ultra-violet rays. In the cooler lands of Europe, pale or freckled skin was more suitable. Later, some of these people moved from their homelands and settled in other parts of the world. They had partners of different appearance from themselves. The children they produced inherited features from both parents.

World faiths

From the earliest times, humans have tried to make sense of their lives. Many have come to believe in spirits, gods, goddesses, or a single God. Others are atheists, with no religious beliefs at all. We have all developed a sense of morality—a code that determines which human behavior is "good" and which is "bad." Leading world religions today include Christianity, Islam, Hinduism, Buddhism, Sikhism, and Judaism. Although these faiths have different forms of worship, they still share many similar values. In the Jewish faith, the Bar Mitzvah celebrates the point at which a 13-year-old boy becomes a man.

Dress and display

Many people, like this dancer from the Indonesian island of Bali, take pride in their traditional clothes and jewelry. Although people around the world often wear similar jeans, T-shirts, suits, or dresses, clothing still varies with a person's job, or the climate. Cool, loose robes are best in hot places, and thick, warm garments in cold areas. Regional costumes are worn for special ceremonies or dances.

Let's talk!

At least 6,000 different languages are spoken around the world. In Ecuador, people speak Spanish and also use indigenous (native) languages, such as Quechua and Jivaro. The world's commonest language, which is spoken by about 1.1 billion people, is Standard Chinese. English is the world's most widespread language.

Housing and shelter

The first humans lived in caves, shelters, or huts made from branches. Today, many people still live in simply constructed dwellings, like these cave houses in Turkey. Housing styles vary greatly from one region to another, depending on local building materials such as stone, clay, timber, or reeds. With the spread of manufacturing, transportation, and engineering technology, many of the world's towns and cities now have similar buildings, made of brick, concrete, steel, and glass.

Social organization

This Papua New Guinea costume shows the wearer's importance in the community. Most societies are divided into groups such as families, age groups, clans (people sharing common descent), or castes (people with the same occupations and social standing). Some groups reflect economic and political power. Others are based on shared culture.

Arts and crafts

Aboriginal peoples have made rock paintings at Australia's Kakadu National Park for more than 20,000 years. Humans seem to share a delight in creating beautiful and artistic pictures, and also in crafting fine objects, whether in pottery, textiles, or wood, like this Indonesian carver. Art and craft styles have varied through time, and from one culture to another, but they can be appreciated by almost everyone.

HOW WE SURVIVE

All humans need food and shelter to survive. We must make a living by farming, selling, making things, or providing services to others. Very few people still live by hunting, fishing, and gathering their own food. The way in which people organize their work, trade, and money is called the economy. Economic activities affect the natural world in many ways—by using up metals and fuels, by changing land use, and by polluting the air, soil, and water.

Some nations are wealthy. They have plentiful resources and trading opportunities. Other nations remain desperately poor, however hard their people may work. Some have few resources or poor soil, and others suffer from droughts or floods. Their governments are forced to borrow money from richer nations, which leaves them heavily in debt. Countries may also be made poor by war, by bad government, or by unfair trading agreements. People living in poorer countries may be forced to work for much lower wages than people in more developed regions of the world. Economic pressures decide not just whether individuals are rich or poor, but whether they are healthy, whether they receive schooling, how many children they might have, and even how long they will live.

The Producers

Wheat (Millions of tons per year)		Rice (Millions of tons per year)		Oil (Millions of barrels per day)		Coal (Millions of tons per year)	
China	113.9	China	198.48	Saudi Arabia	8.595	China	1,118.12
European Union	96.1	India	134.233	U.S.	7.76	U.S.	1,099.12
India	70.0	Indonesia	52.919	Russia	6.18	India	327.98
U.S.	62.7	Bangladesh	32.298	Iran	3.55	Australia	320.59
Russia	31	Vietnam	31.435	Mexico	3.345	Russia	276.31

Farming, fishing, and food

The green pastures of New Zealand, created by grazing sheep, show how farming has been changing the surface of our planet for 10,000 years. Vast natural grasslands, such as the prairies of North America, the pampas of South America, or the steppes of Eastern Europe, are now taken over by crops or cattle. Swamps have been drained. Rivers have been diverted to water farmland. One machine does the work that once employed dozens of people. In wealthy countries, farming is a massive and high-technology business. Yet small producers in poor countries can hardly grow enough for their own families. Also, modern farming is not always efficient. One acre of soy plants yields 22 times more healthy protein than one acre grazed by beef cattle.

Exploitation of forests

Natural resources such as oil, coal, iron, and phosphates are sometimes mined from forested areas. Forests also provide timber for building, fuel, or paper-making. In well-managed forests, care is taken to ensure that trees cut down for timber are replaced, by planting new ones. However, large areas of the world's tropical rain forest are being destroyed by settlements, farming, or mining. If future generations are to enjoy the Earth's riches and wildlife, we must safeguard these precious resources.

Environment

A villager sifts through debris after a flood in Papua New Guinea—more evidence that floods and storms are on the increase in many parts of the world. They destroy crops, buildings, and lives. Many scientists blame this problem on climate change. They believe global warming is the result of polluting the atmosphere with gases from factory chimneys and car exhausts. Floods are worsened by stripping forests from hillsides, as soil and riverbanks are more easily washed away by rain.

Service industries

In the world's richer countries, relatively few people work in factories, construction, or farming. More and more people work in service industries, providing services for others. They might be employed in hotels, restaurants, hospitals and health care, telephone call centers, stores, and government centers. Others have jobs in finance, at banks, or insurance companies. Workers at the New York Stock Exchange buy and sell stocks (shares in businesses). If the business does well, the stockholder (the owner of the stock) is paid part of the profits.

Manufacturing

All over the world, people are coming to depend on mass-produced or manufactured goods such as cars, computers, refrigerators, furniture, and clothes. Although these factory-made items make life easier for those who can afford them, some products and production methods have greatly damaged the environment.

Employers

Many big companies set up factories in places where wages and costs are low. A single product, like a car, may have parts made in many different countries. By operating in this way, some private companies have accumulated so much wealth that they are richer and more powerful than small nations.

NATIONS & GOVERNMENTS

A nation is a part of the world ruled by a government. Some nations are huge, others tiny. Sometimes nations split into smaller ones or unite into bigger ones, and new borders are agreed.

A region with its own government is an independent state. One governed by another country is a dependency or overseas territory. The people of a nation are its citizens. In a democracy, citizens vote for their government. In a monarchy, the king or queen is the ruling head of state. In a republic, the head of state is an elected president.

Systems of government

India is a republic and the world's biggest democracy, with more than half a billion voters. The government has two sections, or houses. Each region or state sends representatives to the Rajya Sabha, House of the States. Members of the Lok Sabha, or House of the People, are elected directly by the public from different political parties.

1 GUATEMALA
2 BELIZE
3 HONDURAS
4 EL SALVADOR
5 NICARAGUA
6 COSTA RICA
7 PANAMA
8 JAMAICA
9 HAITI
10 DOMINICAN REPUBLIC
11 PUERTO RICO
12 ANTIGUA AND BARBUDA
13 ST. KITTS-NEVIS
14 DOMINICA
15 ST. LUCIA
16 BARBADOS
17 ST. VINCENT AND THE GRENADINES
18 GRENADA
19 TRINIDAD AND TOBAGO
20 VENEZUELA
21 GUYANA
22 SURINAME
23 FRENCH GUIANA
24 SENEGAL
25 THE GAMBIA
26 GUINEA-BISSAU
27 GUINEA
28 SIERRA LEONE
29 LIBERIA
30 IVORY COAST
31 GHANA
32 TOGO
33 BENIN
34 EQUATORIAL GUINEA
35 CAMEROON
36 CENTRAL AFRICAN REPUBLIC
37 REPUBLIC OF CONGO
38 RWANDA
39 BURUNDI
40 MALAWI
41 SWAZILAND
42 LESOTHO
43 ERITREA
44 DJIBOUTI
45 ISRAEL
46 JORDAN
47 LEBANON
48 SYRIA
49 KUWAIT
50 BAHRAIN

51 QATAR
52 UNITED ARAB EMIRATES
53 BELGIUM
54 LUXEMBOURG
55 SWITZERLAND
56 NETHERLANDS
57 GERMANY
58 CZECH REPUBLIC
59 AUSTRIA
60 SLOVAKIA
61 HUNGARY
62 SLOVENIA
63 CROATIA
64 BOSNIA-HERZEGOVINA
65 FEDERAL REPUBLIC OF YUGOSLAVIA
66 ROMANIA
67 MOLDOVA
68 ALBANIA
69 MACEDONIA
70 BULGARIA
71 RUSSIA
72 LITHUANIA
73 LATVIA
74 ESTONIA
75 GEORGIA
76 ARMENIA
77 AZERBAIJAN
78 BHUTAN
79 BANGLADESH
80 MYANMAR
81 LAOS
82 THAILAND
83 CAMBODIA
84 BRUNEI
85 SINGAPORE

Political parties

At this rally in Mexico, people who share political views work together in their political party in order to gain power or bring about change. Some parties may support big business and finance, while others support the interests of ordinary working people. Some parties may be against democracy, others are for it. Some may be based on religious beliefs, others are not. In a democracy, the party which wins the most votes at an election forms the next government.

ICELAND SWEDEN FINLAND NORWAY RUSSIA UNITED KINGDOM DENMARK IRELAND 74 73 71 72 BELARUS 56 53 57 POLAND 54 58 60 UKRAINE FRANCE 55 59 61 66 67 KAZAKHSTAN MONGOLIA 63 64 65 70 PORTUGAL SPAIN ITALY 68 69 75 UZBEKISTAN KYRGYZSTAN N. KOREA JAPAN GREECE 76 77 TURKMENI- STAN TAJIKISTAN S. KOREA TUNISIA CYPRUS 47 48 AFGHANI- CHINA MOROCCO TURKEY 45 46 IRAQ IRAN STAN TAIWAN ALGERIA LIBYA EGYPT 49 PAKISTAN 78 WESTERN SAHARA SAUDI 50 NEPAL 51 ARABIA 52 INDIA 79 MAURITANIA OMAN 80 MALI NIGER 43 YEMEN 81 VIETNAM BURKINA CHAD SUDAN 44 82 24 FASO 25 27 NIGERIA 83 PHILIPPINES MARSHALL 26 28 30 31 ETHIOPIA SRI ISLANDS 29 35 36 LANKA 84 32 33 UGANDA SOMALIA MALAYSIA 34 85 GABON 37 THE DEM. KENYA MALDIVES REP. OF 38 CONGO 39 TANZANIA SEYCHELLES INDONESIA PAPUA NEW GUINEA ANGOLA 40 MOZAM- VANUATU ZAMBIA BIQUE MAURITIUS ZIMBAB- NAMIBIA WE BOTS- MADAGASCAR AUSTRALIA WANA 41 SOUTH 42 AFRICA NEW ZEALAND

Miles
0 2,000
0 3,200
Kilometers

Flags and emblems

Flags are used as national badges. The Australian flag includes the Union Flag (to show Australia's historical connection with Britain), the stars of the Southern Cross in the night sky, and a big star to represent states and territories. Australians who wish to break ties with the British monarchy have designed their own unofficial flag, and so have the nation's Aboriginal people.

United Nations

Friendly nations often join together to form groups called alliances. These are usually based on common interests such as trade, politics, religion, or military defense. The biggest alliance, the United Nations

(UN), has most countries in the world as its members. The aim of the UN is to secure a more peaceful, healthier, and fairer world. UN forces may be sent to keep the peace in trouble spots and war zones around the world.

NORTH AMERICA

North America is the world's third-largest land mass, stretching from the icy Arctic Ocean to warm, tropical waters. The southern section is known as Central America—a narrow hook of land that borders the island chains of the Caribbean Sea and is joined to the continent of South America. North America has numerous huge population centers, including Mexico City and New York City, and many large towns. Although regions like the prairie grasslands have been taken over by farming, there are still vast areas of wilderness where few people live.

There are many different theories about how and when North America was first settled. Most experts agree that between 20,000 and 12,000 years ago, when North America was linked to Asia by a bridge of land, bands of hunters crossed into Alaska from Siberia. Their descendants spread out across the continent, and by 3,200 years ago, they were farming and building towns in Mexico. Other hunters, ancestors of the Inuit people, settled in the Arctic. Europeans reached North America, too—

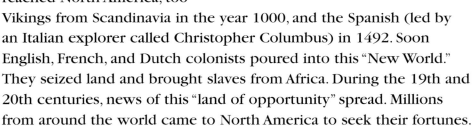

Many peoples

About 800 years ago, Mesa Verde was a settlement of the Anasazi, a Native American people. It was built into a cliff in Colorado, where it can still be visited. Today, the Native American people are outnumbered by those of European, African, Asian, and mixed origins. Such a range of people speak many different languages, including English, French, and Spanish.

Vikings from Scandinavia in the year 1000, and the Spanish (led by an Italian explorer called Christopher Columbus) in 1492. Soon English, French, and Dutch colonists poured into this "New World." They seized land and brought slaves from Africa. During the 19th and 20th centuries, news of this "land of opportunity" spread. Millions from around the world came to North America to seek their fortunes.

Population

The population of the North American continent, including Central America and Caribbean islands, is about 478 million people. Los Angeles and the surrounding area of California is home to 11 million people. The city itself is a center of industry and commerce, specializing in films and television production. Other North American centers of population include the northeastern coast of the U.S., from Boston to New York and Philadelphia; a belt along the southern Great Lakes, including Chicago, Detroit, and Cleveland; and the densely populated region around Mexico City.

Farms and forests

The U.S. has some of the world's most productive farmland, with dairy cattle grazed in Wisconsin and beef cattle ranched in Texas. The prairies produce vast amounts of wheat and other grain crops. California grows citrus fruits and grapes for wine, and cotton is planted in the southern states. Tropical crops of Mexico, Central America, and the Caribbean include bananas, sugarcane, and coffee. Canadian forests provide timber for saw mills.

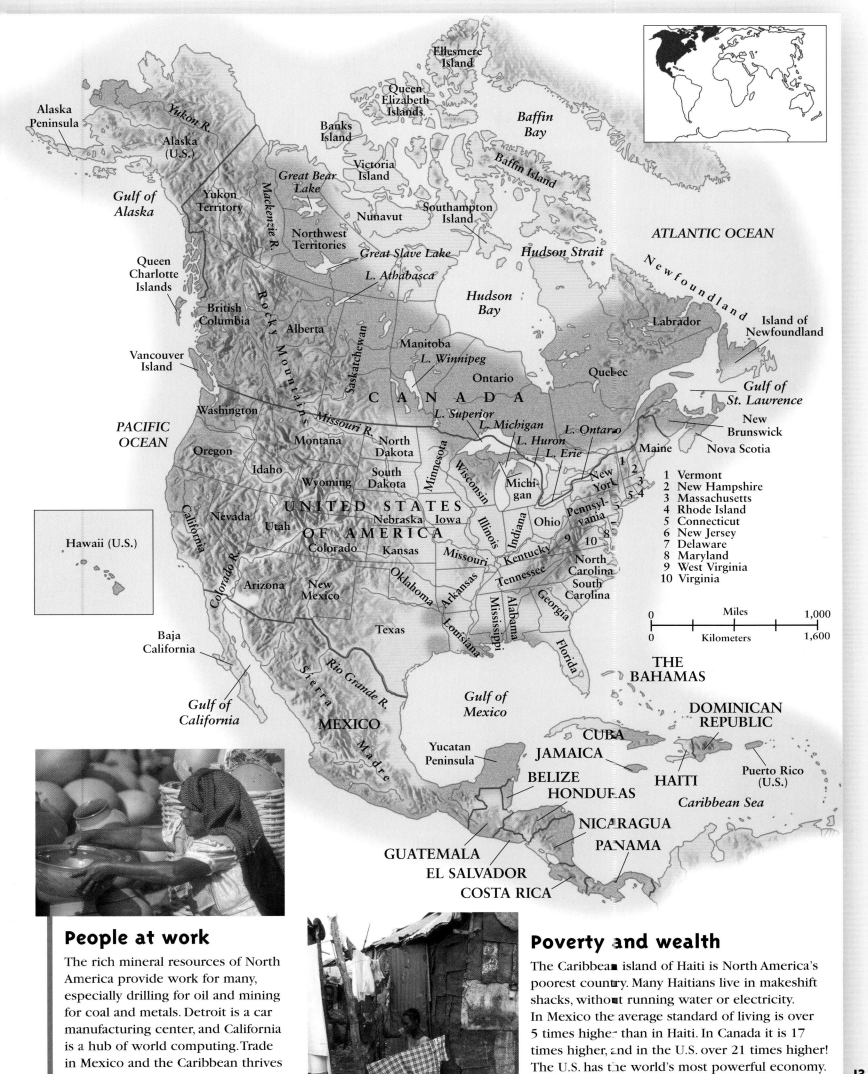

Alaska Peninsula

Yukon R.

Alaska (U.S.)

Gulf of Alaska

Yukon Territory

Mackenzie R.

Great Bear Lake

Banks Island

Victoria Island

Ellesmere Island

Queen Elizabeth Islands

Baffin Bay

Baffin Island

Queen Charlotte Islands

British Columbia

Northwest Territories

Great Slave Lake

Nunavut

Southampton Island

Hudson Strait

ATLANTIC OCEAN

Newfoundland

L. Athabasca

Hudson Bay

Labrador

Island of Newfoundland

Vancouver Island

Alberta

Saskatchewan

Manitoba

L. Winnipeg

Ontario

Quebec

Gulf of St. Lawrence

Rocky Mountains

C A N A D A

Washington

Missouri R.

North Dakota

Minnesota

L. Superior

L. Michigan

L. Huron

L. Ontario

L. Erie

Maine

New Brunswick

Nova Scotia

PACIFIC OCEAN

Oregon

Montana

Idaho

Wyoming

South Dakota

Nebraska

Wisconsin

Michigan

New York

Iowa

Illinois

Indiana

Ohio

Pennsylvania

1   Vermont
2   New Hampshire
3   Massachusetts
4   Rhode Island
5   Connecticut
6   New Jersey
7   Delaware
8   Maryland
9   West Virginia
10 Virginia

California

Nevada

Utah

UNITED STATES OF AMERICA

Colorado

Kansas

Missouri

Kentucky

West Virginia

Virginia

North Carolina

Hawaii (U.S.)

Colorado R.

Arizona

New Mexico

Oklahoma

Arkansas

Tennessee

Mississippi

Alabama

Georgia

South Carolina

Texas

Louisiana

Florida

Baja California

Sierra Madre

Rio Grande R.

Gulf of California

MEXICO

Yucatan Peninsula

Gulf of Mexico

THE BAHAMAS

CUBA

JAMAICA

DOMINICAN REPUBLIC

HAITI

Puerto Rico (U.S.)

Caribbean Sea

BELIZE

HONDURAS

NICARAGUA

PANAMA

GUATEMALA

EL SALVADOR

COSTA RICA

Miles
0 — 1,000
Kilometers
0 — 1,600

People at work

The rich mineral resources of North America provide work for many, especially drilling for oil and mining for coal and metals. Detroit is a car manufacturing center, and California is a hub of world computing. Trade in Mexico and the Caribbean thrives on visiting tourists who buy local produce and souvenirs.

Poverty and wealth

The Caribbean island of Haiti is North America's poorest country. Many Haitians live in makeshift shacks, without running water or electricity. In Mexico the average standard of living is over 5 times higher than in Haiti. In Canada it is 17 times higher, and in the U.S. over 21 times higher! The U.S. has the world's most powerful economy.

13

CANADA & GREENLAND

Few people live in the harsh North American Arctic— a land of ice, tundra, and conifer forests. Most choose to live far to the south, where the climate is milder.

Greenland, the world's largest island, boasts one of the harshest climates. Its small populations live in coastal towns or remote settlements, and are of Inuit, mixed, or Danish descent. Most people rely on fishing for income. Greenland is a self-governing territory of Denmark. The tiny islands of Saint Pierre and Miquelon are French territories.

Canada, an independent country, is the giant of the north. In area, it is the second biggest country in the world. Yet its population is smaller than that of California in the U.S. Canada is a major producer of zinc, uranium, nickel, oil, and gas. Timber and wheat are exported, but falling catches have shut down Newfoundland's fisheries. The Saint Lawrence Seaway links Ontario with the Atlantic, and on the west coast, the chief Pacific seaport is Vancouver.

The Mounties

Canada has a famous police force known as the "Mounties"—Royal Canadian Mounted Police. It was founded as the Northwest Mounted Police in 1867, to bring law and order to the wild lands of the frontier. Heroic stories were told of Mounties who trekked across the wilderness on horseback to "get their man" and bring criminals to justice. The red tunics and broad-brimmed hats of that age are still worn for ceremonial parades, but for everyday work, Mounties now wear modern uniforms.

The city of Toronto

On the shores of Lake Ontario, the port of Toronto is the capital of Ontario province. It is the biggest city in Canada and an important center of communications, commerce, finance, and manufacturing. Toronto is largely English-speaking, with a population of about 5 million. Many people are of English or Scottish descent. There are also Jewish, Italian, Greek, Chinese, and Afro-Caribbean communities.

Calgary Stampede

The Calgary Stampede is Canada's most famous rodeo. Here you can see flying hooves and tossing horns, wagon races, and competitions in traditional cowboy skills. The festival has been held since 1912, when Calgary, Alberta, was the one of the chief cattle-market towns on the North American prairies. The city later became wealthy through the discovery of oil. Today it is a business center with a population of 740,000. But the cowboy way of life is still very much the reality in rural parts of southern Alberta.

Canada
Cap: Ottawa
Pop: 31 million
Area: 3,849,674 sq mi
(9,970,610 sq km)

GREENLAND

CANADA

Greenland
(Denmark)
Cap: Nuuk (Godthåb)
Pop: 56,000
Area: 840,000 sq mi
(2,175,600 sq km)

Peoples of Canada and Greenland

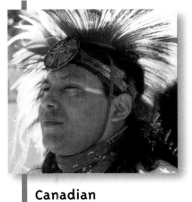
Canadian

Greenlander

About 625,000 Canadians are descended from the earliest inhabitants of the country, known today as the "First Peoples" or "First Nations." They include the Innu, Micmac, Mohawk, Cree, Blackfoot, Ojibwe, Kwakiutl, and various Déné cultures. Small communities of Inuit are scattered along the coasts of the Canadian Arctic and Greenland. The French explored and settled in Canada in the 1600s, and today about 6.7 million Canadians, mostly in Quebec, claim French as their first language. English and Scots also settled the region beginning in the 1600s, and today English is the first language of a majority of Canadians. However, both English and French are official languages throughout Canada. Some French-Canadians have campaigned for the Province of Quebec to break away from Canada and become a separate French-speaking nation, but they have been unsuccessful.

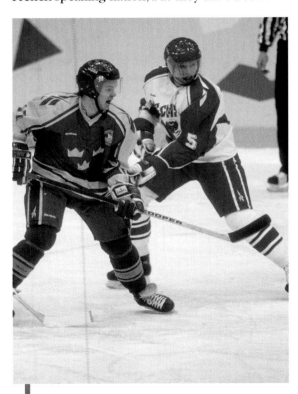

Ice hockey

Although Canada has many languages and cultures, it is united in its love of ice hockey. This fast, furious sport originated in Canada in the 1800s, and has since gained an enthusiastic following in the U.S., Russia, and around the world. L-shaped sticks are used to send the puck skidding across the ice rink. Each team has five players and a goalkeeper. Both Canadian and U.S. teams compete in the National Hockey League.

Travel in the snow

Canada has heavy winter snowfall and the thaw arrives late in spring. In the past, winter travel in Canada had to be by horse-drawn sleigh or, in the far north, by dog sled. Today, snowmobiles make travel almost as easy as by motorcycle. They are used throughout the Arctic over short distances. Light aircraft with landing skis are used for longer journeys to remote communities.

Maple syrup

Buckets and tubes are used to collect the sap of the sugar maple, a tree which is grown in the Canadian provinces of Ontario, Quebec, and New Brunswick. The sap is boiled until it forms a sweet, sticky syrup. The maple syrup is then served with pancakes, ice cream, and other dishes. The leaves of the maple tree turn brilliant shades of gold, red, and orange, before they drop every fall, to color the woodlands of North America. A maple leaf is Canada's emblem, appearing on the national flag.

Inuit furs

In Nunavut, the Canadian territory which is homeland for the Inuit people, winter temperatures of −27°F (−33°C) combine with the wind-chill factor to cause frostbite in seconds. Traditional clothes were made from skins and furs of caribou (North American reindeer), seals, Arctic foxes, hares, and polar bears. These were stitched into shirts, leggings, trousers called kamiks, coats, hoods, gloves, and boots. Today's Inuit may still wear these for a hunting trip, but stores offer modern garments like waterproof padded jackets. The future may bring great changes to the Arctic way of life. Global warming is causing the big freeze to arrive later and the spring melt to begin earlier.

15

NORTH AMERICA

The United States of America (or the U.S.) is the world's third-largest country by area. It is also an economic giant, and in terms of military might, the most powerful nation on Earth.

The northeastern and midwestern U.S. have many great population centers. These include New York, Chicago, Boston, Philadelphia, Cleveland, St. Louis, and Minneapolis–St. Paul. The Industrial Revolution in the U.S. happened first in the Northeast, as cities grew up along the rivers, which provided water power for early factories. Heavy industries such as steel-making have declined in many places, but enormous factories like the automobile plants of "Motor Town"—Detroit, Michigan—still exist. Lake Michigan lies entirely within the U.S. The other four Great Lakes straddle the Canadian border, with access to the Atlantic Ocean via the Saint Lawrence Seaway.

The midwest is drained by the vast Mississippi-Missouri river system as it flows southward. In the 1800s, European settlers seized the prairie grasslands of the Great Plains from the Native American people. Today, a vast patchwork of farmland spreads across the prairies, with numerous cattle ranches in the west. Yet a few areas of natural grassland still survive.

The "Big Apple"

New York City, nicknamed the "Big Apple," sprawls over islands and shores at the mouth of the Hudson River. It is the biggest city in the U.S. and has a brash character and highly charged energy all of its own. On the central island of Manhattan, office workers and yellow taxi cabs fill the busy streets, dwarfed by high skyscrapers. Manhattan is a center of finance, advertising, and entertainment. Other city boroughs include the Bronx to the north, Staten Island, and Queens and Brooklyn, both to the east on Long Island. The city's most famous landmark, the Statue of Liberty, was a gift from France in 1886. It towers over the approaches to New York Harbor.

United States of America
Cap: Washington D.C.
Pop: 284.5 million
Area: 3,615,104 sq mi
(9,363,130 sq km)

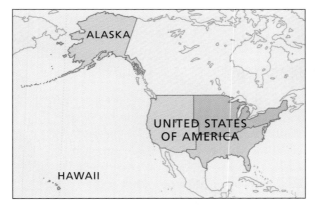

Boston, Massachusetts

The seaport of Boston has played an important part in American history. Boston's people were among the first to reject British taxation in the late 1700s. The city was later settled by many Irish and Italians. Boston is famous for such New England dishes as Boston baked beans, lobster, and codfish.

Peoples of the northeast and midwest

North Dakotan

Iowan

The first people to settle in the region were Native Americans. They included the Iroquois of the northeast, and hunters of the Great Plains, such as the Sioux, Plains Cree, and Blackfoot. Early European arrivals included the English and Dutch, who settled along the Atlantic coast, and the French, who made their homes around the Great Lakes and the waterways of the Mississippi–Missouri river system. Later settlers came from all over Europe, with many Irish, Scots, Germans, Italians, Poles, and Russians. In the early 20th century, African-Americans migrated from the south U.S. to cities in the northeast and midwest, where they could find employment and faced less discrimination. Immigration from Mexico and other Spanish-speaking lands in the Caribbean and Central America grew rapidly in the late 1900s. Most recently, many immigrants have arrived from Southeast Asia and Russia.

New England

The northeastern region of New England is made up of six small states— Maine, New Hampshire, Vermont, Massachusetts, Rhode Island, and Connecticut. Although New England includes large industrial areas, it also has some of the most beautiful scenery in the U.S., from the Atlantic breakers of Maine's Acadia National Park to the highland regions of the Green and White Mountains. Woods of birch and maple turn beautiful colors during fall. English colonists, known as the "Pilgrim Fathers," founded Plymouth Colony in Massachusetts in 1620. The region still has many historic houses and churches from the 1600s and 1700s, and such prestigious universities as Yale (in New Haven) and Harvard and the Massachusetts Institute of Technology (MIT), both in Cambridge.

Food for the nation

Dairy cattle are raised for milk and cheese production on the green pastures of New York State and the lakeside states of Wisconsin and Minnesota. The prairies of North America stretch westward across the Great Plains and northward across the Canadian border. They have become one of the world's great food-producing regions. Huge areas are planted with wheat, corn, soy beans, and vegetables. Beef cattle are ranched in the west.

Chicago life

Commuters are carried above the streets of Chicago by an elevated railway known as the "El." The city's skyscrapers soar above Lake Michigan and the rolling prairies to the west. Chicago has a fascinating past. It is famous for its criminals of the 1920s and for its part in the history of the Blues, the emotional music brought to the city by African-Americans. Today, Chicago is famous for modern architecture and its finance markets, which trade in minerals, crops, and fuels. Among Chicago's attractions are two major league baseball teams—the Cubs and the White Sox.

U.S.: THE SOUTH

The south of the U.S. runs from the sandy shores of the mid-Atlantic coastline to the humid Gulf of Mexico.

The wooded Appalachian Mountain ranges run northeast from Alabama through Virginia and into the Northeastern States. The great flood plain of the Mississippi River lies to the west, spilling over a broad delta before meeting the sea. In late summer and fall, hurricanes batter the Gulf coast with waves and high winds. Westward again lies the huge state of Texas, where the Rio Grande forms the frontier with Mexico.

The south's warm climate makes it possible to grow crops such as tobacco, cotton, sugarcane, peanuts, and pecans. Stretching south toward the Caribbean, the Florida peninsula's warm climate produces oranges and grapefruit. Many hotels and retirement homes have been built here because of the area's year-round sunshine. Cape Kennedy is famous as the launch site of many space missions. Texas is cattle ranching country, where high boots and Stetson hats are worn not only by cowboys, but also by business people working in the state's rich oil industry.

District of Columbia

The District of Columbia (D.C.) is the site of the U.S. capital, Washington. It is built beside the Potomac and Anacostia rivers. Washington is a city of 600,000 people. It is not part of any state, although its suburbs sprawl across neighboring state lines. The city center has broad avenues, green spaces, and many imposing but low-rise buildings. The Capitol building is the seat of the U.S. Congress, and the White House is the official home of the President. The Lincoln Memorial honors Abraham Lincoln, the president who led the northern states through the Civil War. He helped defeat the pro-slavery southern states, but was assassinated days after the south's surrender.

New Orleans

New Orleans, the biggest city in Louisiana, is on the wide and slow-flowing Mississippi River. In the 1800s, it was a port of call for steamboats driven by great paddle wheels at the stern, as they transported passengers and goods up and down the river. Today, the boats carry tourists. New Orleans is built in a low-lying region, protected from floods by high banks called levees. The climate is hot and sticky, and thunderstorms are common. French settlers founded the city in 1718, then Spain ruled from 1763 to 1803, until Louisiana was purchased by the U.S. The old city center, with its pretty courtyards and balconies, is known as the French Quarter, or Vieux Carré. Each spring it hosts the colorful Mardi Gras carnival. Jazz music began in New Orleans around 1900. The south has given birth to many kinds of music, from Mississippi Delta blues to the Cajun dance music of Louisiana.

MARYLAND
WEST VIRGINIA
DELAWARE
KENTUCKY
OKLAHOMA   ARKANSAS
VIRGINIA
TENNESSEE
NORTH CAROLINA
SOUTH CAROLINA
TEXAS
GEORGIA
ALABAMA
MISSISSIPPI
LOUISIANA
FLORIDA

Peoples of the south

Tennessean

Alabaman

Native American peoples of the south include the Seminole, Choctaw, and Creek. Oklahoma has the highest proportion of Native Americans of any state, since many groups were moved there in the 1800s. European colonists included English and Scots in the north and east, and Spanish and French to the south. In the 1700s, many French-Canadian refugees, known as Cajuns, settled in Louisiana. In recent years, Cubans have arrived in Florida, and Mexicans in Texas. African-Americans were first brought to the south as slaves in the 1600s. Their descendants were freed in 1865, but faced over a hundred years of struggle to gain their full rights as American citizens.

The Old Dominion

Founded in 1607, Virginia is often known as the "Old Dominion." This state includes England's first successful colony on the Atlantic coast. Its settlers became wealthy landowners, who prospered growing tobacco on plantations. They built grand mansions as their crops were worked by slaves, who had been shipped in horrific conditions mainly from Africa. Industries today include agriculture and tourism, and the state has a major naval base and port for Atlantic shipping at Hampton Roads.

King Cotton

The U.S. is the world's second largest cotton producer. Cotton plants are grown across the south, from Georgia to Texas. The cotton plant's fluffy seed head, or boll, contains the fibers that are used to make cotton thread or yarn. This is woven into textiles for garments ranging from T-shirts to fine dresses. Cotton was once picked by hand, but today much of the hard work is done by machines.

Kentucky home

The state of Kentucky is known for its whiskey, fried chicken, and its coal mines. It is also famous for its racehorses, which are raised around Lexington on rich pastures, where a type of grass called bluegrass thrives. America's most famous horse race is the exciting Kentucky Derby. It takes place at the beginning of May at Churchill Downs, near the city of Louisville.

In the Everglades

Florida has one of the world's biggest wetland areas, made up of the Everglades and the Big Cypress Swamp. Shallow pools are filled with sawgrass, beardgrass, and water lilies, and dotted with small islands named hummocks, where cypress trees are festooned with creepers and mosses. The wetlands support an amazing variety of animal wildlife, including alligators, diamondback rattlesnakes, egrets, bald eagles, a peaceful plant-eating mammal called the manatee (sea cow), and rare tree snails. The Everglades are a major tourist attraction, but they are endangered by draining, farming, pollution, and the spread of towns.

U.S.: THE WEST

NORTH AMERICA

The western part of the U.S. borders the vast Pacific Ocean, and includes Alaska and the Pacific islands of Hawaii.

The Rocky Mountains run southward from the Canadian border to form a high, snow-capped barrier. To the east are the prairies, a grassland area where cattle are grazed. To the west lies the Great Basin, a strange landscape of eroded rocks, salt lakes, and deserts, which extend from the southwest U.S. across the Mexican border. The highest Rocky Mountains are in Colorado, which draws many tourists who come to enjoy its beautiful scenery or to enjoy winter sports such as skiing. Tourists also flock to Las Vegas, in the Nevada desert, for entertainment, lavish hotels, and gambling.

The southwestern states are farmed with the help of irrigation, and also produce minerals such as copper, gold, silver, lead, and uranium. Between the mountain ranges and the ocean are densely populated areas, with forested regions to the north. California is the most productive agricultural state in the U.S. It is a center of business, manufacturing, film, television, and computing. Hawaii is a very popular tourist spot and grows tropical crops such as pineapples.

Arctic Alaska

The U.S. purchased Alaska from Russia in 1867. It became a state (the largest in the U.S.) in 1959. Most people live along the southern coasts, where the climate is often moist and foggy. The interior and north are bleak, mountainous, empty, and usually icy. Here, winters are long and summers are very short. The economy depends largely on fisheries, timber, and oil, which is piped from Prudhoe Bay in the far north to the port of Valdez on the southern coast.

San Francisco

The California city of San Francisco was founded by the Spanish in 1776. It lies beside the blue waters of San Francisco Bay and the Pacific Ocean. The climate of this beautiful city can change in minutes, from warm and springlike to cool and shrouded in fog. Like many parts of the Pacific coast, the region has suffered over the years from severe earthquakes. Old-fashioned cable cars climb the city's steep hills. A rapid transit system and road bridges, including the spectacular Golden Gate bridge, provide easy access to population centers around the bay.

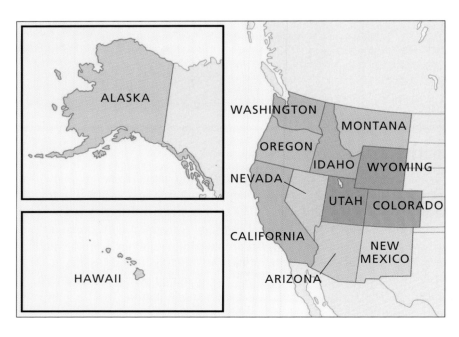

ALASKA

WASHINGTON

MONTANA

OREGON

IDAHO   WYOMING

NEVADA

UTAH   COLORADO

CALIFORNIA

NEW MEXICO

HAWAII   ARIZONA

Peoples of the western U.S.

Californian   Hawaiian

Arctic peoples of the western states include the Aleuts and the related Inuit groups of Alaska. Native American peoples once lived throughout Alaska and the states to the south. Today, their cultures remain strong in the northwest and southwest, which is the home of the Navajo and Apache. People of European descent in the region include English and Irish. Others have Mexican origins, with Hispanic (Spanish or part-Spanish) roots. Many African-Americans live in the region, especially in the Los Angeles area. Long-standing Asian communities include Japanese-Americans and Chinese-Americans, whose center is the "Chinatown" district of San Francisco. Hawaiians are one of the Polynesian peoples of the Pacific islands.

Western trails

In 1849, gold was discovered in California. Thousands of hopeful travelers made the long journey across the continent to stake their claims. Very few got rich, but many stayed, beginning years of rapid growth. By the 1960s the state had more people than any other, and today it is more populous than Australia or Canada. Today's city-dwellers relive the pioneers' sense of adventure by exploring the state's giant sequoia and redwood forests, or by riding on horseback through its canyons and valleys.

Grand Canyon

The Grand Canyon, in the state of Arizona, is a huge gash in the Earth's surface—one of the great natural wonders of the world. It has been carved out of solid rock by the flowing waters of the Colorado River over the past few million years. The canyon drops to a depth of almost a mile (1,600 m) and ranges from 4 to 12 miles (6–20 km) wide. Its entire length stretches for 200 miles (320 km), with about 100 miles (160 km) in Grand Canyon National Park. Many visitors hike along its rims, and some make the long trip by trail to the river below.

Whale watching

Whaling was a traditional livelihood for peoples of the Pacific, providing meat, and fats and oils to burn for light, warmth, and cooking. Today, only native peoples of the northwest are allowed to kill whales, and only in limited numbers. However, whale-watching has become an important new attraction. People pay to board boats and watch these magnificent creatures migrate between the Arctic and their tropical breeding waters. Species seen include gray, humpback, and right whales.

THE TROPICS

NORTH AMERICA

North America's southern regions include Mexico, the smaller nations of Central America, and the Antilles island chain in the Caribbean Sea.

Mexico is a large country with richly varied landscapes of deserts, mountains, plains, and tropical forests. It lies within an earthquake and volcano zone. The north is cattle ranching country, while the high plains grow corn, wheat, and beans. Mexico is rich in minerals and is the world's fifth-largest oil producer. Its capital, Mexico City, is a gigantic industrial center on the Central Plateau. Mexico is also a vacation destination, and its beaches attract many tourists.

Central America has mountains and tropical forests, and the Caribbean islands are bedded in volcanic rock and coral. Peaceful seas often turn violent during the fall hurricane season. Many people live by fishing or growing tropical crops such as coffee, sugarcane, bananas, tobacco, and cotton, but poverty is widespread in the region.

Ancient sites

Great civilizations developed long ago in Mexico and Central America. By 2300 B.C., pottery was in existence, by 1200 B.C., towns were built, and by 800 B.C., a form of writing was in use. Remains of great civilizations dot the Yucatán peninsula, with ruins of many cities, temples, and statues. The people who created these cultures were the Olmecs, Zapotecs, Maya, Toltecs, and lastly the Aztecs. Built on a lake island, the Aztec capital of Tenochtitlán was captured by Spanish invaders in 1521 and then ruined. Mexico City now occupies the same area.

Mexico
Cap: Mexico City
Pop: 99.6 million
Area: 761,400 sq mi
(1,972,545 sq km)

Cuba
Cap: Havana
Pop: 11.3 million
Area: 42,803 sq mi
(110,862 sq km)

Haiti
Cap: Port-au-Prince
Pop: 7 million
Area: 10,710 sq mi
(27,750 sq km)

Dominican Republic
Cap: Santo Domingo
Pop: 8.6 million
Area: 18,700 sq mi
(48,440 sq km)

Belize
Cap: Belmopan
Pop: 300,000
Area: 8,865 sq mi
(22,965 sq km)

Honduras
Cap: Tegucigalpa
Pop: 6.7 million
Area: 43,265 sq mi
(112,085 sq km)

Jamaica
Cap: Kingston
Pop: 2.6 million
Area: 4,411 sq mi
(11,425 sq km)

Other Caribbean nations and dependencies

Anguilla (U.K.)
Antigua and Barbuda
Aruba (Netherlands)
Bahamas
Barbados
Cayman Islands (U.K.)
Dominica
Grenada
Guadeloupe (France)
Jamaica
Martinique (France)
Montserrat (U.K.)
Netherlands Antilles (Netherlands)
St. Kitts-Nevis
St. Lucia
St. Vincent and the Grenadines
Trinidad and Tobago
Virgin Islands—British (U.K.)
Virgin Islands—U.S. (U.S.)

MEXICO
CUBA
BELIZE
JAMAICA
HONDURAS
GUATEMALA
EL SALVADOR
COSTA RICA
NICARAGUA
PANAMA
HAITI
DOMINICAN REPUBLIC
PUERTO RICO

Guatemala
Cap: Guatemala City
Pop: 13 million
Area: 42,030 sq mi
(108,890 sq km)

El Salvador
Cap: San Salvador
Pop: 6.4 million
Area: 8,260 sq mi
(21,395 sq km)

Costa Rica
Cap: San José
Pop: 3.7 million
Area: 19,130 sq mi
(50,900 sq km)

Nicaragua
Cap: Managua
Pop: 5.2 million
Area: 50,193 sq mi
(130,000 sq km)

Panama
Cap: Panama City
Pop: 2.9 million
Area: 29,761 sq mi
(77,082 sq km)

Puerto Rico (U.S.)
Cap: San Juan
Pop: 3.9 million
Area: 3,460 sq mi
(8,960 sq km)

Peoples of the tropics

Mexican

Trinidadian

The indigenous (native) peoples in many parts of Mexico and Central America are cousins of U.S. Native Americans. They make up 40 percent of the population in Guatemala, and 20 percent in Mexico. They include the Tarahumara, Nahua, Huastec, Zapotec, and Maya. Spanish, English, Irish, French, Dutch, and other Europeans settled in the region after the 1500s. Many Caribbeans and Central Americans are of Spanish descent, and mestizos (people of mixed Spanish-indigenous descent) form the majority of the population. Afro-Caribbeans are descendants of Africans brought to the region as slaves in the 1500s, but who gained their freedom in the 1800s. They now form a majority on most Caribbean islands, and there are minorities on the mainland's Caribbean coastline. The Garifuna of Belize are of African-indigenous descent.

Tourist dollars

Many tourists who wish to escape the colder weather of Western Europe and North America enjoy the tropical climate of Mexico, Central America, and the Caribbean. Among the attractions are palm-fringed beaches and warm seas, sport fishing and scuba diving, visits to historical sites and, increasingly, the chance to experience the wealth of wildlife in the rain forests. Although tourism brings much-needed money and employment to poor regions, the building of hotels and swimming pools sometimes threatens the natural environment. Tourist developments may also be cut off from local communities. Visitors can visit vacation destinations without ever experiencing the reality of day-to-day life in the Caribbean.

Bananas and beans

Busy markets are at the center of daily life in Mexico and Central America. Tropical fruits, tomatoes, squashes, and vegetables are laid out in crates or on sheets and rugs, or piled up high on stalls in village squares. The foods of the region are often highly spiced with chili peppers. Rice, beans, and cornflour pancakes known as tortillas are the basis of many meals. Eggs, cheese, chicken, beef, and fish are also common ingredients. Mexican cooking is now popular in many cities around the world.

Weaving

The craft traditions of indigenous peoples in Central America date back to ancient times. Maya women in Guatemala weave textiles of the finest quality on backstrap looms, to make traditional blouses called huipils, shirts, skirts, and belts. All textiles are brilliantly colored with natural dyes, but the traditional patterns vary from one village to another. Treasured designs and motifs include the Aztec feathered serpent-god of arts and crafts, Quetzalcoatl.

SOUTH AMERICA

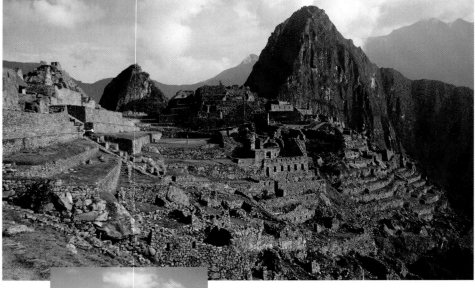

The South American continent is the fourth largest in the world. It is bordered by the southern Atlantic and Pacific Oceans, and is joined to North America by a narrow land bridge, or isthmus. The mountain range of the Andes stretches the entire length of the continent, forming a chain of icy peaks and high plateaus. To the east are the mighty Orinoco and Amazon rivers, threading their way through the world's largest rain forests. The northeastern Guiana Highlands drop toward the hot and humid Caribbean coast. In the southern half of the continent there are areas of thorny scrub, deserts, river valleys, fertile farmland, grasslands, and the bleak, cold, windy region of Patagonia in the far south. The land mass tapers to a point at Cape Horn, where stormy waters stretch all the way to Antarctica.

Humans have adapted to life in all parts of South America. Some still survive in the ancient ways, as they hunt wild animals and gather plants in the green gloom of the rain forests. Others grow potatoes and herd llamas in the high Andes, where the air is thin and cold. The people of the continent are descended from prehistoric North American settlers, who migrated south over many centuries and spread across the varied landscapes. European peoples, especially the Spanish and Portuguese, also settled in almost all areas after the 1500s. They founded the major cities that exist today.

Land of the Incas

From 4,500 years ago until the Spanish conquest of 1532, great civilizations sprang up in the Andes and along South America's Pacific coast. One of the best-preserved settlements is the ancient town of Machu Picchu, in Peru. Clinging to the side of a mountain, 9,000 feet (2,743 m) above sea level, it was constructed by the ancient Incas. Five hundred years ago, the Inca Empire stretched almost the length of South America, from Colombia to Chile. Fortunately, many marvellous Inca buildings have survived.

Cities and slums

South America's biggest cities are Rio de Janeiro and São Paulo, both situated on the Atlantic coast of Brazil. More than three-quarters of all Brazilians are town-dwellers, and the number increases daily as poor country people move to the cities in search of work. Unable to afford the high rents for smart apartments, they live in shantytowns called *favelas*—unhealthy slums of makeshift shacks, with no clean water supplies or proper sanitation. The population of São Paulo has soared to more than 18 million.

Buenos Aires

Buenos Aires is the capital of Argentina. Its name means "fair breezes," and it has attracted European settlers for over 450 years. The city is a port on the south bank of the Rio de la Plata, or Plate River. It is densely populated, with 40 percent of all Argentinians living there, rather than in the remote countryside. Buenos Aires made its wealth from the export of beef, but today it is also a center of business, industry, communications, and the arts.

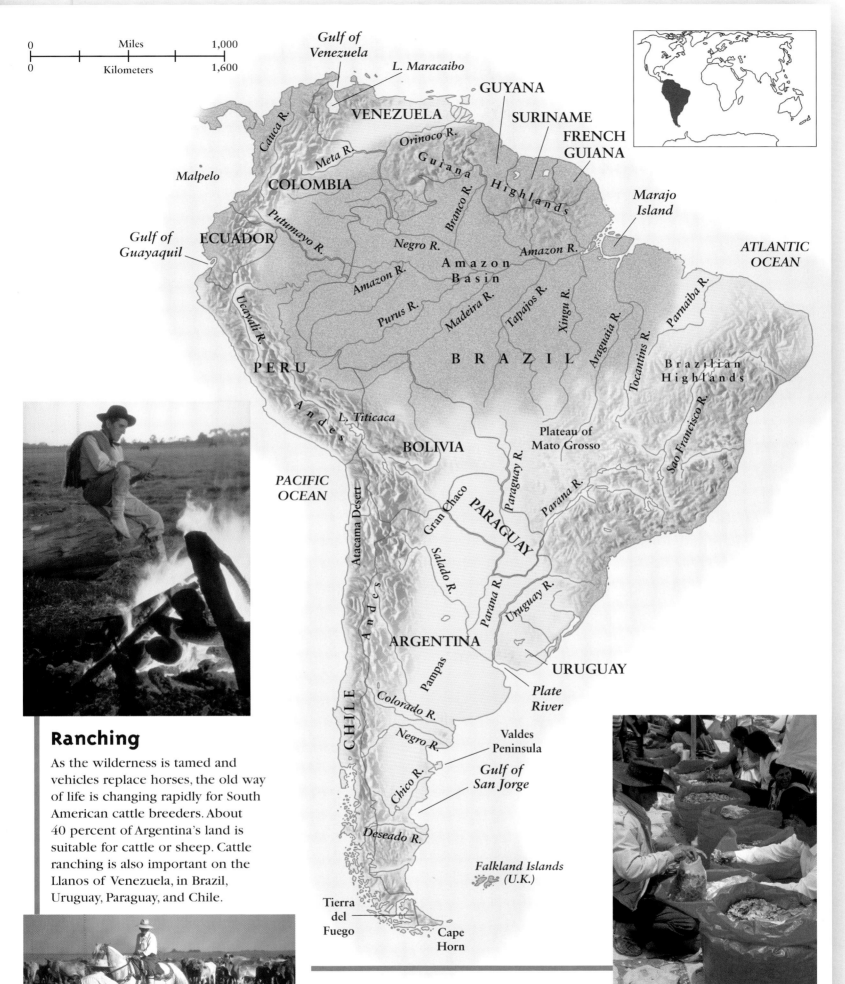

Scale:
| 0 | Miles | 1,000 |
| 0 | Kilometers | 1,600 |

Gulf of Venezuela
L. Maracaibo
GUYANA
VENEZUELA
SURINAME
FRENCH GUIANA
Cauca R.
Orinoco R.
Meta R.
Guiana Highlands
Malpelo
COLOMBIA
Marajo Island
Putumayo R.
Branco R.
Gulf of Guayaquil
ECUADOR
Negro R.
Amazon R.
ATLANTIC OCEAN
Amazon R.
Amazon Basin
Ucayali R.
Amazon R.
Purus R.
Madeira R.
Tapajos R.
Xingu R.
Araguaia R.
Parnaiba R.
PERU
B R A Z I L
Brazilian Highlands
Tocantins R.
Andes
L. Titicaca
São Francisco R.
Plateau of Mato Grosso
BOLIVIA
PACIFIC OCEAN
Paraguay R.
Parana R.
Gran Chaco
PARAGUAY
Parana R.
Atacama Desert
Salado R.
Andes
Parana R.
Uruguay R.
ARGENTINA
URUGUAY
Pampas
Plate River
Colorado R.
CHILE
Negro R.
Valdes Peninsula
Chico R.
Gulf of San Jorge
Deseado R.
Falkland Islands (U.K.)
Tierra del Fuego
Cape Horn

Ranching

As the wilderness is tamed and vehicles replace horses, the old way of life is changing rapidly for South American cattle breeders. About 40 percent of Argentina's land is suitable for cattle or sheep. Cattle ranching is also important on the Llanos of Venezuela, in Brazil, Uruguay, Paraguay, and Chile.

Market day

In many parts of South America, poor families only grow enough crops for their own needs. Any leftover produce is traded at local markets, loaded onto stalls or in rows of baskets. Chilies, tomatoes, potatoes, and corn were first grown in the Americas and were carried to other parts of the world in the 1500s. Markets offer a chance for country people to meet and exchange news and gossip, as well as to trade.

THE NORTHWEST

The snowy Andes Mountains rise high in Colombia and stretch southward. Steamy rain forests lie to the east, while arid plains and fertile valleys border the Pacific.

Colombia has coastlines on both the Pacific Ocean and the Caribbean Sea. Poverty is widespread in the country, and many families travel from their homes to big cities such as Bogotá, Medellín, and Cali in search of work. The nation's resources include oil, coal, and hydroelectric power. Crops include coffee and coca, a leaf that is illegally processed and exported as the drug cocaine.

Bananas are the main crop in Ecuador, the smallest of the Andean nations. "Ecuador" is the Spanish word for "Equator"—the line of latitude that crosses the country to the north of the capital, Quito.

In Peru, large fishing fleets operate along the coasts and out in the Pacific. Cotton and sugar are grown on the plains. Types of grain and potato that thrive at high altitudes are grown on terraced fields on the Andean mountainsides.

Across the high, deep waters of Lake Titicaca lies Bolivia, the region's most sparsely populated nation. It has twin capital cities at Sucre and La Paz (the world's highest city). Bolivia exports tin, gold, silver, oil, and natural gas, as well as timber.

Music of the Andes

Traditional Andean folk musicians play a type of pan-pipes called *zampoñas* or *antaras*, as well as flutes, drums, and guitars. Some of their haunting melodies date back more than 500 years to the festivals and ceremonies of the Inca Empire. All have been strongly influenced by the music of Spain, which ruled the whole region for nearly 300 years. Today, the music of the Andes has influenced pop and folk music worldwide.

Reeds from the lake

Tough reeds called *totora* grow around the shallow margins of Lake Titicaca, on the Peruvian–Bolivian border. The villagers who live around the lakeshore and on its islands cut the reeds and use them to make roof thatch, matting, and baskets. The totora reeds are also bound into tight bundles to make small fishing boats called *balsas*. When still tender, the young shoots of the *totora* may be harvested and eaten.

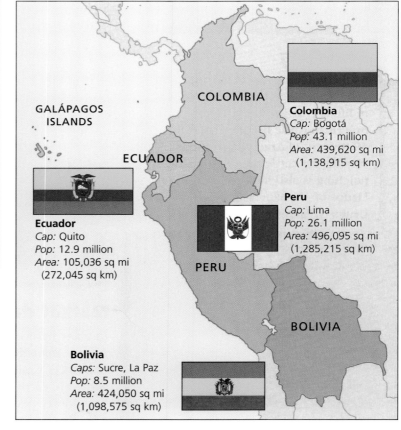

GALÁPAGOS ISLANDS

COLOMBIA

Colombia
Cap: Bogotá
Pop: 43.1 million
Area: 439,620 sq mi
(1,138,915 sq km)

ECUADOR

Ecuador
Cap: Quito
Pop: 12.9 million
Area: 105,036 sq mi
(272,045 sq km)

Peru
Cap: Lima
Pop: 26.1 million
Area: 496,095 sq mi
(1,285,215 sq km)

PERU

BOLIVIA

Bolivia
Caps: Sucre, La Paz
Pop: 8.5 million
Area: 424,050 sq mi
(1,098,575 sq km)

Peoples of the northwest

Peruvian

Colombian

Many indigenous peoples still live in the northwest of South America. They include the Páez, Guambiano, Kogi, Gaujiro, and Otavaleños. The largest ethnic groups in the region are the Quechua and Aymara highlanders of Bolivia and Peru. Afro-Caribbeans live on Colombia's northern coast, mostly in Cartagena and Barranquilla. Other people of African descent live in the Pacific lowlands and in northern Ecuador. Today, many families are of European descent. Most of these are Spanish—in fact, Spanish is the main language spoken throughout the region today. The greatest part of the regional population (about 58 percent in Colombia) is of mixed or mestizo (European-indigenous) descent. There are also small Asian communities in the region, which are mainly of Chinese and Japanese origin.

Useful llamas

Four members of the camel family are found in South America. They all have long, flat backs, upright necks, and small heads. Llamas are generally used to carry goods along tracks high in the Andes, and for their wool, hides, and meat. The llama is sure-footed, but can show a foul temper if its load is too heavy. The alpaca is herded mainly for its wool, which is shorn every two years. The wild vicuña is also prized for its coat, which provides yarn of the finest quality. The guanaco is another wild relative, which lives only on lower slopes and plains. It is thought that llamas were bred from wild guanacos more than 5,000 years ago.

Derby hats

The Aymara people live in the mountains and high plateaus of Bolivia and Peru. Aymara market women wear the type of round hat known as a derby. The hat was probably introduced to the region in the early 20th century by British railroad workers. It has since been adapted to local designs and materials.

Lord of the Miracles

Some 95 percent of all people in the northwest of South America are followers of the Roman Catholic faith. Every October, about 2 million Christians flock to Lima, the capital of Peru, to celebrate the feast of the Lord of the Miracles. During the ceremony, men dressed in purple robes carry a shrine through the streets. It is said to be a copy of a painting of Christ on the cross, made on a wall hundreds of years ago by an African slave. The painting has survived various disasters, including several earthquakes in the 1600s, and is believed to possess miraculous powers.

Color and cloth

The Tsáchila are a small group of indigenous people who live in Ecuador. In Spanish they are known as *Colorados*, because they color their bodies and hair with an orange-red dye obtained from the seeds of a plant called achiote. Various other indigenous peoples in the region, such as the Waorani, also adorn themselves with paint and feathers. Andean indigenous groups wear beautifully woven hats, ponchos, or shawls, often made from llama wool. As in other parts of the world, standard Western-style dress is becoming more common.

THE NORTHEAST

SOUTH AMERICA

South America's northeast is a land of two great rivers, the Orinoco and Amazon, with the world's biggest rain forest, other amazing natural features—and the largest cities, too.

Venezuela borders the Caribbean Sea and the oil-rich shallows of Lake Maracaibo. A branch of the Andes drops into a broad central plain crossed by the Orinoco River. The forested Guiana Highlands run east into Guyana, Suriname, and French Guiana, three small countries that produce tropical crops such as sugarcane and bananas.

To the south lies Brazil—a huge nation that occupies the Amazon basin as well as highlands, plateaus, and plains. Brazil mines gold, silver, and iron, and manufactures steel. Coffee and sugar are grown on a massive scale. The continent's biggest cities, São Paulo and Rio de Janeiro, are on the Atlantic coastline. In the interior, the survival of one of the world's most precious resources, the Amazonian rain forest, is constantly threatened by development.

Guyana
Cap: Georgetown
Pop: 700,000
Area: 82,980 sq mi
(214,970 sq km)

Suriname
Cap: Paramaribo
Pop: 400,000
Area: 63,235 sq mi
(163,820 sq km)

Venezuela
Cap: Caracas
Pop: 24.6 million
Area: 352,050 sq mi
(912,045 sq km)

French Guiana
(France)
Cap: Cayenne
Pop: 200,000
Area: 35,125 sq mi
(91,000 sq km)

Brazil
Cap: Brasília
Pop: 171.8 million
Area: 3,285,620 sq mi
(8,511,965 sq km)

Carnival

Carnival is held each year in February or March, before the Christian fast of Lent. It is celebrated more in Brazil, and especially in Rio de Janeiro, than anywhere else in the world. Hundreds of thousands of people take to the streets during the festival, where they sway to the samba, a rhythmic dance that originated in Africa. There are parades of floats, which are vehicles covered with fantastic decorations. Revelers dress in glittering, spectacular costumes that take all year to make.

Rivers, roads, and airstrips

The Amazon basin is drained by a vast maze of small rivers and streams that feed the great river itself. Many villages are situated on the riverbanks. Canoes and motorboats are still the easiest way to travel through these densely forested lands, although the rain forest's new roads and airstrips are opening it up to miners, loggers, and farmers. This development involves the destruction of huge numbers of trees, and in some areas it is disastrous—

not only for the environment, but for indigenous peoples. The new settlers persecute them, bring diseases against which they have little resistance, destroy their hunting grounds, and poison the rivers and lakes.

Peoples of the northeast

Guyanan

Brazilian

Indigenous peoples of South America's northeast include the Guajiro, Warao, and Piarora in Venezuela, and Brazilian groups such as the Kayapo, Xavante, and Yanomami. People of mixed indigenous-European descent are known as mestizos, Mestiços, or Caboclos. People of African descent also live throughout the region, including Bush Negroes or Marrons, whose ancestors escaped slavery in the Guianas. The region was formerly ruled by European nations—Venezuela by the Spanish, Brazil by the Portuguese, and the Guianas by the British, Dutch, and French. The languages of these nations remain the major ones of the region. Immigrants to Brazil have included Germans, Italians, and Poles, and there is a large Japanese community. Other Asians descended from workers who came to Guyana and Suriname in the 1800s include Indians, Chinese, and Javanese.

Capoeira

About 400 years ago, African slaves in Brazil invented capoeira. It is a martial art, a game, a dance, and an acrobatic display—all at the same time! Capoeira is performed in a circular space called the roda. The combatants perform leaps and cartwheels, as musicians and singers accompany the action. The traditional version of capoeira is called "angola." The more modern version, known as "regional," is faster but shorter.

Cassava

Cassava, also known as manioc or tapioca, is a shrub with swollen, starchy roots called tubers. It is grown as a food crop throughout the tropics, but is native to South America. Cassava is widely grown in the Amazon River basin and can be harvested at any time of the year. The tubers are peeled, pressed (to squeeze out poisons contained in the plant), and grated or ground into meal called farinha. The meal is boiled and mashed to eat.

City people

Brazil's capital, Brasília, was built in the 1960s on the country's central plain. Unlike this modern capital, with its futuristic buildings of concrete, steel, and glass, Brazil's enormous Atlantic cities were founded long ago, in the days of Portuguese rule. People from Rio de Janeiro are known as Cariocas, while those from São Paulo are called Paulistas. Although many people who work in the major business and finance centers have become wealthy, there are also growing numbers of young orphans who struggle to make a living as gangs of "street children."

Soccer heroes

Popular throughout South America, soccer is a way of life, especially in Brazil. The sport is played on beaches, on city streets, and in countless clubs. Brazilian national teams have repeatedly been world-beaters. Pelé (born in 1940) is often rated the best player the world has ever seen, and became a great world ambassador for the game.

THE SOUTH

SOUTH AMERICA

Other than major cities and some fertile farmland in milder regions, southern South America is thinly populated.

Most Paraguayans live in the east of their country, between the Paraguay and Paraná rivers, where cotton and soy beans are grown. To the west lies the sparsely populated Gran Chaco region. Cattle graze the grasslands of Uruguay, which stretch east to the Atlantic coast. Montevideo, on the north shore of the Plate River, is a major industrial center.

On the river's south shore is the port of Buenos Aires, the capital of Argentina. This large country exports beef, wool, oilseeds, and wine. Chile is a long, narrow nation. Although the north is mainly desert, it is rich in minerals, and the fertile central region produces apples and grapes. The capital, Santiago, is located here. The maze of islands and channels at the continent's southern tip are cold and stormy.

The Maca

The lands of the Maca people once stretched far to the west of the Paraguay River. Today, only about one thousand of these indigenous people remain, within a reservation near Asunción. Most live by selling craft items to tourists in the city—a story all too common in the southern regions of South America. Countless indigenous peoples, from the Gran Chaco to Tierra del Fuego, have been destroyed in the last 200 years. Certain groups, such as the Mapuche of Chile, offered fierce resistance. Some of these peoples were murdered or destroyed by disease and alcohol. Other indigenous groups were forcibly resettled as European colonists seized their lands.

Gaucho lore

Gauchos, the cowboys of Argentina, are famed in folk tales for being tough, daring horseback riders with their own code of honor. Although old ways of life are fading, gaucho costumes (including hats, belts, and boots) are still worn at country festivals. Even city people like to imagine themselves as part of the gaucho tradition.

Chile
Cap: Santiago
Pop: 15.4 million
Area: 290,125 sq mi
(751,625 sq km)

Easter Is.
(Chile)

Paraguay
Cap: Asunción
Pop: 5.7 million
Area: 157,005 sq mi
(406,750 sq km)

Uruguay
Cap: Montevideo
Pop: 3.4 million
Area: 68,038 sq mi
(176,221 sq km)

Argentina
Cap: Buenos Aires
Pop: 37.5 million
Area: 1,072,240 sq mi
(2,777,815 sq km)

CHILE PARAGUAY

URUGUAY

ARGENTINA

FALKLAND IS. (U.K.)

Peoples of the South

Argentine

Paraguayan

The indigenous groups of Paraguay, Uruguay, and Argentina include the Guaraní, Mataco, and Toba. Another indigenous people, the Mapuche, number about 800,000 in Chile. The first Europeans to settle the region were the Spanish, who arrived here in the 16th century. Even today, Spanish is still the dominant language of the area. Later arrivals included the English and the Scots, who made the Falkland (Malvinas) Islands a British colony. Mainland settlers included Welsh, Germans, Danes, Dutch, Belgians, Swiss, Italians, Poles, Russians, and Hungarians. People of mixed European-indigenous ancestry are known by the Spanish term mestizos ("mixed"). The Asian communities include Turks, Syrians, and Lebanese, along with Koreans and Japanese. Easter Islanders, on one of the world's most remote specks of land, are of Polynesian origin.

A bitter tea

Paraguayan holly is a shrub used to make the traditional tea-like drink *yerba maté*, which is brewed from its crushed and dried leaves. Maté contains caffeine (as found in coffee and tea) and has been used for centuries by native peoples as a pick-me-up. It is often served in a gourd-shaped flask, and drunk through a metal drinking straw and strainer called a bombilla. The drink is popular in Paraguay, Uruguay, and Argentina.

At the world's end

Ushuaia is the world's most southerly town, and home to about 42,000 people. A busy fishing port and naval base, it lies in mountainous Tierra del Fuego. Ushuaia attracts tourists eager to watch penguins and whales, or to explore the bleak but beautiful landscape of the far south. The port is also a departure point for voyages to Antarctica.

Itaipú dam

The biggest hydroelectric complex in the world is the Itaipú dam, which is operated jointly by Paraguay and Brazil. The dams hold back the waters of the Paraná River to create a reservoir with an area of some 521 sq miles (1,350 sq km). The turbines can generate 12.6 MW (megawatts) of electricity. The dams cost 25 billion American dollars to build, placing a great strain on the economies of the region. However, the power plant, which began generating in 1984, provides Paraguay with almost all of its electricity needs, and even allows the country to export electrical power at a profit.

Southern sports

The game of polo did not originate in South America. However, it has gained a following in Argentina, a land with a long tradition of skilled horsemanship. Here, those who can afford to breed and keep the fine horses required for polo indulge in the sport. Other Argentinian sporting passions include soccer, rugby football, and motor racing. Perhaps the greatest racing driver ever, Juan Manuel Fangio (who raced in the 1950s), was Argentinian, and the national soccer team won the Football World Cup in 1978 and 1986. Outdoor pursuits, such as skiing, canoeing, or hiking in the Andes Mountains, are also popular.

EUROPE

Europe is a great wedge of land that stretches from the North Atlantic Ocean eastward to the Ural Mountains. It is part of the larger land mass called Eurasia. In the far north, Europe borders the icy waters of the Arctic Ocean. In the northwest, it forms the Scandinavian peninsula and extends to the British Isles. Southwestern Europe borders the warm Mediterranean Sea, whose northern shore is formed by the Iberian, Italian, and Balkan peninsulas. Southeastern Europe borders the Black Sea and the Caucasus Mountains, with Asia beyond.

Europe's far north has an Arctic climate, with bitter winters. An ocean current called the North Atlantic Drift warms many of the northwestern coasts, which have milder, moister weather. Far from the sea, parts of Central and Eastern Europe have cold, snowy winters, but warm summers. Southern Europe is mild in winter and hot and dry in summer. Many European countries enjoy high living standards, with more and more joining the European Union (EU), a powerful economic and political alliance. European nations were the first to become industrial powers and the first to build up worldwide empires. Much of the region is densely populated and developed, with few remaining areas of natural wilderness.

Prehistoric Europe

Cave paintings found at sites such as Altamira in Spain and Lascaux in France show that humans have inhabited Europe for tens of thousands of years. The pictures show that, as the climate warmed after the last Ice Age, the animals which people hunted also changed. Farming skills entered Europe from the Near East about 7,000 years ago.

Civilizations

The great civilizations of ancient southern Europe still inspire us today. More than 2,500 years ago, the ancient Greeks, followed later by the Romans, developed an awe-inspiring understanding of science, engineering, politics, mathematics, art, poetry, music, and theater. The Romans conquered much of Europe, the Near East, and North Africa. They built aqueducts (water channels, many on bridges) to carry water through the dry lands.

Fishing fleets

Fishing has been a way of life in coastal Europe for thousands of years. Northern fleets from Iceland, Norway, The Netherlands, and the British Isles caught cod and herring, while Mediterranean fleets fished for tuna and sardines. Fishing remains an important industry, but scientists fear that overfishing, warmer waters, and industrial pollution are threatening the future of many fish stocks. This worry has forced the EU to place limits on catches.

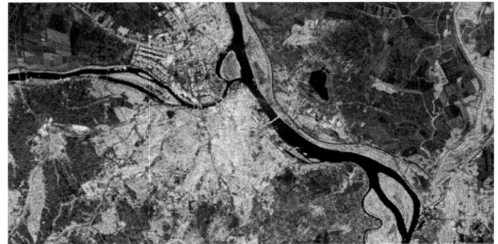

Cities and people

A satellite in space takes a picture, which is then computer-enhanced. This one shows how the city of Belgrade has grown up around the Sava and Danube rivers. The capital of Yugoslavia, Belgrade's inhabitants number 1.6 million. The total European population of 727 million is gradually declining. About 73 percent of Europeans live in towns or cities.

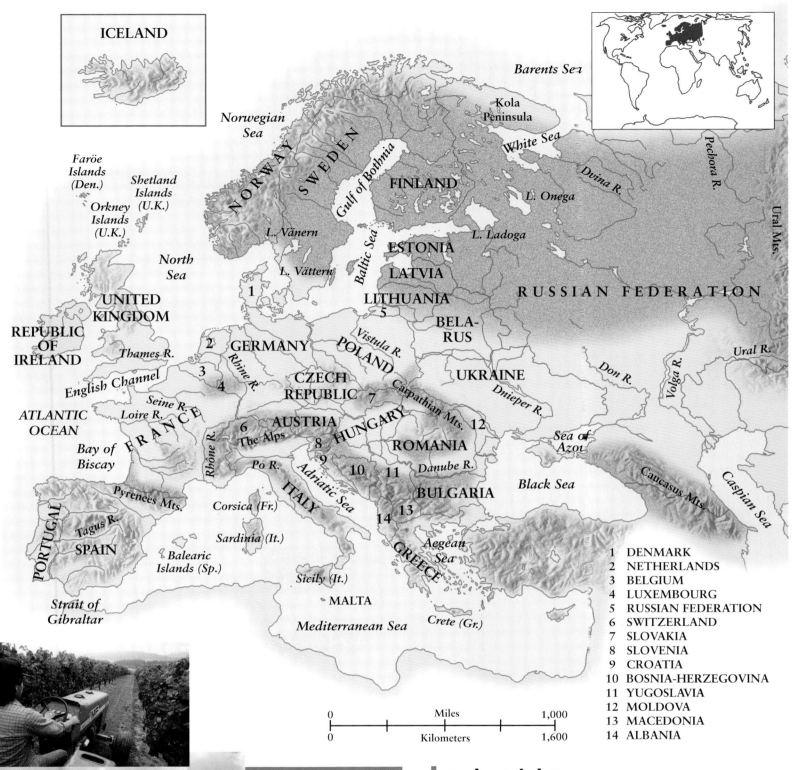

ICELAND

Norwegian Sea

Barents Sea

Kola Peninsula

White Sea

Duina R.

Pechora R.

L. Onega

NORWAY

SWEDEN

FINLAND

Gulf of Bothnia

L. Vänern

Baltic Sea

L. Vättern

L. Ladoga

ESTONIA

LATVIA

LITHUANIA

Ural Mts.

Faröe Islands (Den.)

Shetland Islands (U.K.)

Orkney Islands (U.K.)

North Sea

UNITED KINGDOM

1

5

BELA-RUS

RUSSIAN FEDERATION

REPUBLIC OF IRELAND

Thames R.

2 GERMANY

POLAND

Vistula R.

UKRAINE

Ural R.

English Channel

3

4

Rhine R.

CZECH REPUBLIC

7

Carpathian Mts.

12

Don R.

Dnieper R.

Volga R.

Seine R.

Loire R.

FRANCE

6

The Alps

AUSTRIA

HUNGARY

8

Sea of Azov

ATLANTIC OCEAN

Bay of Biscay

Rhône R.

Po R.

9

10

11

ROMANIA

Danube R.

Caucasus Mts.

Caspian Sea

Adriatic Sea

ITALY

BULGARIA

Black Sea

PORTUGAL

Pyrenees Mts.

Corsica (Fr.)

14

13

SPAIN

Tagus R.

Sardinia (It.)

GREECE

Aegean Sea

1   DENMARK
2   NETHERLANDS
3   BELGIUM
4   LUXEMBOURG
5   RUSSIAN FEDERATION
6   SWITZERLAND
7   SLOVAKIA
8   SLOVENIA
9   CROATIA
10 BOSNIA-HERZEGOVINA
11 YUGOSLAVIA
12 MOLDOVA
13 MACEDONIA
14 ALBANIA

Balearic Islands (Sp.)

Sicily (It.)

Strait of Gibraltar

MALTA

Mediterranean Sea

Crete (Gr.)

0	Miles	1,000
0	Kilometers	1,600

Farmland

In prehistoric times, large areas of Europe were thickly forested. European farmers cleared much of the woodland to develop agriculture in fertile regions. The steppe grasslands of Ukraine have rich, black soil where grain crops such as wheat, barley, and rye are widely grown. These are used mainly to make bread, which is the basis of the European diet. Potatoes, sugar beet, and green vegetables are important crops in the north and east. In the south, grapes, olives, and citrus fruits are produced, but some regions of Spain are in danger of becoming desert.

Industrial Europe

Industries on a large scale were first developed in the British Isles in the 1700s, marking the start of the Industrial Revolution. Steam power, factories, and railroads soon spread across much of Western Europe. In the

20th century, the Soviet Union rapidly became industrialized, followed by its neighbors in Central and Eastern Europe. Recently, heavy industries such as coal-mining, steel-making and shipbuilding have declined. Europe still manufactures vehicles, railroad locomotives, and aerospace products.

33

THE FAR NORTH

EUROPE

The peninsulas and islands of northern Europe make up a region called Scandinavia. This area of land stretches from the freezing Arctic to the milder coasts around the North Sea.

Iceland lies in the North Atlantic, just below the Arctic Circle. It is a bleak, rocky land of volcanoes, warm springs, and geysers that gush up from the depths of the Earth. Most Icelanders live by fishing.

The North Sea provides oil and natural gas as well as fish. Norway is a mountainous country with deep-sea inlets called fiords. Bordering the Baltic Sea, both Sweden and Finland have great forests dotted with thousands of lakes. Farming is possible in the more southerly regions, where the soil is fertile and the summers are warmer. Pigs and dairy cattle are raised on the pastures of Denmark.

Reindeer herders of Lapland

The Saami people, who live in the far north of Scandinavia, herd reindeer (Eurasian version of the North American caribou). Numbering 500 or more, reindeer herds graze on mosses and provide meat, milk, hides, furs, and bones. They are rounded up and driven along traditional migration routes, over distances of up to 225 miles (360 km). In the last 50 years, settlement and industrial development in the far north have restricted the herds' movements. Many Saami have settled in towns and taken other work. Recent mineral discoveries, including oil, coal, and the ore rocks of precious metals, may also threaten the future of the Lapland environment.

Viking heritage

The Vikings lived in Scandinavia between the 700s and the 1100s. They earned their name, which means "sea raider," from the violent forays they made on hundreds of coastal towns and villages all around the North and Baltic Seas. Using their long ships, they journeyed as far as North America, Russia, and the Middle East. Some Vikings stayed and settled in these various regions, including the almost empty lands of Iceland and Greenland.

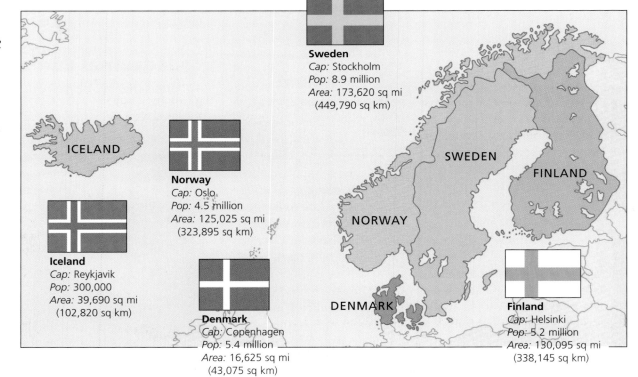

Sweden
Cap: Stockholm
Pop: 8.9 million
Area: 173,620 sq mi
(449,790 sq km)

ICELAND

Norway
Cap: Oslo
Pop: 4.5 million
Area: 125,025 sq mi
(323,895 sq km)

Iceland
Cap: Reykjavik
Pop: 300,000
Area: 39,690 sq mi
(102,820 sq km)

Denmark
Cap: Copenhagen
Pop: 5.4 million
Area: 16,625 sq mi
(43,075 sq km)

Finland
Cap: Helsinki
Pop: 5.2 million
Area: 130,095 sq mi
(338,145 sq km)

SWEDEN

FINLAND

NORWAY

DENMARK

Peoples of the far north

Swede

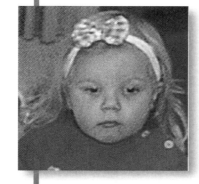

Finn

Finno-Ugric peoples include the Saami, a group that migrated into the region from Russia about 10,000 years ago. The Saami are related to the Finns, who moved into the north Baltic coast region about 2,000 years ago. Saami homeland stretches across the Arctic. The Danes, Swedes, and Norwegians are descended from Germanic peoples who settled in southern Scandinavia 2,000 years ago. Most Icelanders are descended from Norwegian Vikings. Though the Danish, Swedish, Norwegian, and Icelandic people are all related, they speak separate languages. As a result of its rule over Greenland, Denmark has an Inuit community. In common with other European countries, many foreign workers and refugees have recently settled in Scandinavia, including groups from Eastern Europe, South Asia, China, and Japan.

Copenhagen

Developed as a seaport, the Danish capital of Copenhagen was built on the eastern coast of the island of Zealand. It is a center of business, finance, and industry, exporting Denmark's lager-style beers, bacon, dairy products, paper, textiles, and machinery. Copenhagen and its suburbs have a population of approximately 1.5 million. It is a lively city and especially popular with young people.

The Little Mermaid statue, one of its most famous landmarks, is found in the harbor. The statue commemorates the renowned children's author Hans Christian Andersen (1805-75). This celebrated Dane wrote many world-famous folk tales and stories, such as *The Snow Queen*, *The Tin Soldier*, and *The Ugly Duckling*.

Northern churches

Scandinavia was one of the last regions in Western Europe to adopt Christianity, after 960 A.D. About 90 percent of Scandinavians are Protestants, whose faith is reflected in the architectural style of this church at Asmarka, Norway. Many Protestants follow the teachings of the German monk Martin Luther (1483-1546), who led Northern Europe's break with the Roman Catholic Church in 1517.

St. Lucia's Day

As the cold and darkness of the long winter settles over Sweden, the festival of St. Lucia, or Lucy, celebrates the light and warmth which are many months in the future. The festival is held on December 13. A procession is led by a group of girls dressed in white gowns and wearing headdresses of candles and evergreen leaves. The St. Lucia's Day Festival is traditionally the time when the Swedish people start to look forward to the holiday of Christmas.

Snow and ice

Skiing has played a very long and important part in Scandinavian history. An ancient wooden ski found at Hoting in Sweden is believed to date back 4,500 years! Today, many ordinary Scandinavians are expert skiers and ice-skaters. So popular is the sport of skiing that each year, a Nordic (cross-country) ski race called the Vasaloppet takes place. It covers 55 mi (89 km), attracts thousands of competitors, and is the world's biggest Nordic sports event. The race commemorates the start of a successful rebellion by the Swedish people, led by Gustavus Vasa, against the ruling Danes in 1521.

EUROPE

BRITISH ISLES

The British Isles are surrounded by the Atlantic Ocean, the Irish Sea, the North Sea, and the English Channel.

The two largest islands of the British Isles are Great Britain and Ireland. The United Kingdom (U.K.) is a union of the three lands called England, Scotland, and Wales, together with the province of Northern Ireland. The remainder of Ireland forms an independent republic. The British Isles have a temperate climate, with higher rainfall in the west. The landscapes include green fields, moors, peat bogs, low mountains, and seashores. In the 1800s, the U.K. ruled a huge empire and was the world's biggest industrial power, but today it relies more on service industries such as banking and insurance. Ireland exports dairy products. Both the U.K. and Ireland have joined the European Union.

United Kingdom
Cap: London
Pop: 60 million
Area: 94,475 sq mi
(244,755 sq km)

Republic of Ireland
Cap: Dublin
Pop: 3.8 million
Area: 26,895 sq mi
(68,895 sq km)

London

Built around the Thames River, London is the capital of England and of the United Kingdom as a whole. More than 8.6 million people live in the city and its suburbs.
Landmarks include the clock tower of the Houses of Parliament, whose bell is called "Big Ben," and the medieval fortress of the Tower of London. London is a busy city, popular with young people and tourists, and has many famous stores, theaters, museums, and art galleries. The City of London is one of the world's great financial centers.

Getting around

The first roads in England were built by the ancient Romans more than 1,900 years ago. Canals were dug in the 1700s, and the world's first railroads were constructed in the 1800s. Today, England is crossed by an ever-growing network of busy roads, many of them converging on the second biggest city, Birmingham. For a fairly small country, England has a relatively high population, and this places a strain on its road and rail systems. England is linked with France by a 30-mi (50-km) rail tunnel below the Channel.

Country life

Although 90 percent of people in the U.K. now live in towns or cities, the nation still has many associations with the countryside and its traditions. Country people come together during spring and summer at agricultural shows and markets. They may watch cattle or sheep being judged, sheep dogs being put through their paces, or show jumping.

Peoples of the British Isles

English

Irish

The Scots, Irish, Welsh, and Cornish people are of principally Celtic descent and Celtic languages such as Scots Gaelic, Irish, and Welsh are spoken in some regions. The English are mostly a Germanic people, descended from Angles, Saxons, Vikings, and Normans from France. The English language is heard throughout the British Isles and was carried around the world during the age of empire. Many people from the distant countries of the British Empire later came to settle in the U.K. Today, there are large communities of Asians, such as Bengalis and Chinese, and also people of African or Afro-Caribbean descent. Older communities include Jews and Romany (Gypsies). The people of the small, self-governing Isle of Man have Celtic-Scandinavian roots, while many Channel Islanders are of Norman-French origin.

Wales

The Menai Suspension Bridge, an engineering marvel at the time of its construction in the 1820s, crosses the Menai Strait in North Wales. The bridge links the Welsh mainland with the island of Anglesey. Wales borders England to the east, with the Irish Sea to the north and west, and the Bristol Channel to the south. It is a land of estuaries, green valleys, moors, and mountainsides, dotted with flocks of sheep. Heavy industries in the northeast and south, such as coal-mining and steel manufacture, have declined in the last few decades. Wales has its own ruling Assembly at the capital, Cardiff, and is also represented at the U.K. Parliament. About half a million people, mostly in the west and northwest, speak Welsh as their first language. Choral singing and poetry are national passions, as is the game of rugby union football.

Céad Míle Fáilte

This saying means "one hundred thousand welcomes" in the Irish language. Poverty once forced many Irish people to emigrate, but in recent years the Irish economy has flourished. Irish pubs or bars, many of them serving Irish whiskeys and stouts (black beers), are much imitated overseas. Sports include horseracing and hurling, a type of hockey unique to the region.

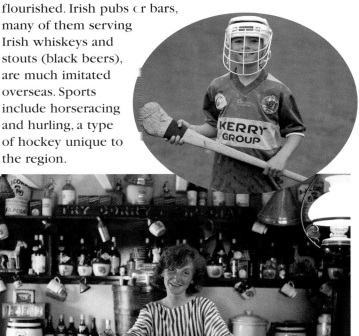

Scotland the brave

Scotland occupies the islands and the mainland to the north of England. Its capital, Edinburgh, surrounds a high rock and castle on the southern shores of the Firth of Forth (estuary of the Forth River). Edinburgh is home to the Scottish Parliament. Scotland also sends members to the U.K. Parliament. Its lowlands include industrial towns and the large, busy city of Glasgow. The wild and beautiful highland region and the islands, which attract many tourists, include remote tracts of countryside and small farms. These places are famous for their salmon and venison (deer meat), and also for their production of Scotch, the "original" whiskey. Aberdeen is a base for offshore oil production in the North Sea.

THE LOWLANDS

EUROPE

Many parts of the North Sea coast lie below sea level. Sea walls and tidal barriers are essential to prevent floods.

The Netherlands is a flat, low-lying country with rivers, canals, and polder (land reclaimed from the sea). Amsterdam and other towns have beautiful brick houses dating from the 1600s. There are also large modern areas, as in the port of Rotterdam. Exports include electrical and household goods, cut diamonds, vegetables, and greenhouse produce. Belgium is also low-lying, but in the south rises to the wooded hills of the Ardennes. Here, too, are beautiful old towns alongside industrial centers. Belgian produce includes beers, cold meats, and chocolates. Tiny Luxembourg is set among vineyards, woods, and farmland. Its capital of the same name is a world center of banking and finance.

Bulbs and windmills

The South Holland region of the Netherlands has to be pumped dry of incoming water in order to be farmed. Traditionally the pumping was powered by tall windmills, whose great sails were kept turning by breezes blowing in from the North Sea. Many old windmills are preserved today as a tourist attraction. One of the region's main crops, the tulip, has been a Dutch obsession since the 1500s. Along with the bulbs of daffodils and other blooms, tulips are still a lucrative business today. Many visitors come to see the colorful flower fields in the spring.

Saxophonics

The Netherlands and Belgium are a long way from the home of jazz music, New Orleans in the U.S. However, jazz has been popular in the region for many years. Indeed, one of the most popular jazz instruments, the saxophone, was invented by a Belgian named Antoine ("Adolphe") Sax (1814-94). Unfortunately, Antoine lived long before the jazz age even began. He also invented a sax-horn and a sax-tuba, but none of his inventions made him a fortune.

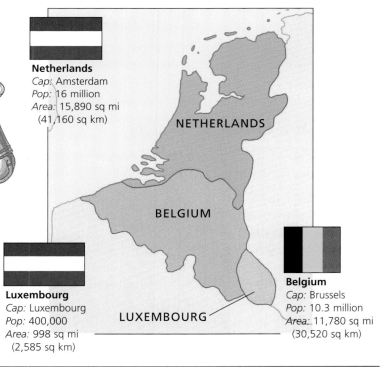

Netherlands
Cap: Amsterdam
Pop: 16 million
Area: 15,890 sq mi
(41,160 sq km)

NETHERLANDS

BELGIUM

Luxembourg
Cap: Luxembourg
Pop: 400,000
Area: 998 sq mi
(2,585 sq km)

LUXEMBOURG

Belgium
Cap: Brussels
Pop: 10.3 million
Area: 11,780 sq mi
(30,520 sq km)

Dutch cheese-making

The towns of Edam and Alkmaar, in North Holland, are famous for their traditional cheese markets, which attract many sightseers. Another cheese-making center is Gouda, in South Holland. Black and white Friesian cows (Holstein) are used for dairy farming in Holland, and dairy produce such as cheeses and butters are among its most important industries. Dutch cheeses are exported all over the world.

Peoples of the lowlands

Dutch

Belgian

Germanic peoples include the Frisians, who have their own language and live both in the north and on the offshore islands. The Dutch make up the majority of the Netherlands population, and are essentially the same people as the Flemings of Belgium. Their language is known as Dutch, or Flemish. The Walloons of Belgium are of mixed Celtic and Germanic descent and are distinguished by speaking French. The Luxemburgers, too, are of mixed descent and speak French or a Germanic speech termed Letzebuergesch. Both Belgium and the Netherlands once had overseas empires and, as a result, have populations of African, Afro-Caribbean, or Asian descent. These include Surinamers and Javanese in the Netherlands and Congolese in Belgium. Over the years, the region has also attracted Turkish workers and their families.

Beside the canals

The Belgian city of Bruges, or Brugge, is capital of West Flanders and a beautiful old city with many fine buildings that date back to the Middle Ages. At that time, Bruges was an important market for the Hanseatic League, an organization of merchants that traded across Germany and eastward to the lands around the Baltic Sea. The Flemings produced the finest textiles in Europe, and Bruges later became famous for its lace-making. Industry was revived in the 1800s and 1900s with the building of a new ship

canal to the coast and the large seaport of Zeebrugge. Bruges is now a center of communications, with an economy that takes in light engineering, brewing, and tourism. Especially popular are the Beguinage, a quiet, peaceful retreat for nuns, and the large medieval belfry and market hall in the old city.

Festival time

Festivals in both Belgium and the Netherlands include many historical pageants and religious celebrations. Among these are the Procession of the Holy Blood, which is held in Bruges each May, and the arrival of St. Nicholas, who is known in the region as Sinterklaas. He is welcomed in Amsterdam each December. Carnival (Shrove Tuesday) is celebrated with parties and parades in South Holland and Belgium.

Brussels, city of Europe

Brussels, the capital of Belgium, has a population of nearly 1 million. One of its most famous monuments, the Atomium, was built for the 1955 World's Fair, and celebrated Europe's rebuilding 10 years after World War II. At that time, Belgium, the Netherlands, and Luxembourg began working toward a united, prosperous Europe. They were among the founding nations of an organization which later became the European Union (EU). Today, as headquarters of the EU Commission, Brussels plays a leading role in both European and world politics.

Luxembourg

Founded in the Middle Ages, Luxembourg is known as a Grand Duchy—an area ruled by a duke or duchess. The whole country is even tinier than Rhode Island, the smallest state in the U.S. Its capital city rises above the Alzette River. Luxembourg originally made its wealth from iron and steel, benefiting from being close to the industrial centers of France, Belgium, and Germany. Today, Luxembourg depends mainly on financial services, such as banking and insurance. These give it the world's highest standard of living, or gross domestic product (GDP) per citizen. Like Brussels, Luxembourg is home to important EU institutions.

FRANCE & MONACO

France is bordered by the English Channel, the Atlantic Ocean, and the Mediterranean Sea. Monaco is an independent city-state on its south coast.

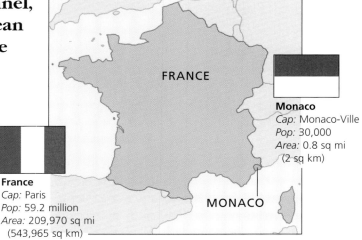

France
Cap: Paris
Pop: 59.2 million
Area: 209,970 sq mi
(543,965 sq km)

Monaco
Cap: Monaco-Ville
Pop: 30,000
Area: 0.8 sq mi
(2 sq km)

Rivers wind through France's flat northern farmlands, with their temperate, moist climate. In the center is the high, rocky Massif Central. Beyond the broad Rhône valley, hills border the east—the Vosges, Jura, and the high, snowy Alps. The west coast runs from Brittany's rocky headlands south to dunes and pine forests, with the Pyrenees as another mountain barrier along Spain's border. The Mediterranean coasts of the south are hot and dry in summer, mild in winter.

France is a founder member of the European Union and has a high standard of living. Many small farms grow wheat, corn, vegetables, apples, and grapes, with exports of wine, butter, and cheese. Industries include vehicle and aircraft manufacture, mining, textiles, and tourism. Through history, France has played a leading role in European politics, literature, music, art, drama, and films.

Height of fashion

Paris can claim to be the leading city of world fashion. As early as the Middle Ages, grand ladies in other European lands were copying and dressing in the French style. In the 1800s, popular magazines revealed all the latest bows, bonnets, and gowns to be worn that year in Paris. In the 20th century, classic dress designers such as Coco Chanel were widely admired. Even today, magazine editors still flock to Paris to see models parade on the runways at fashion shows.

Wining and dining

September is the time of the grape harvest in many parts of France, where some of the world's best red and white wines are produced. The names of grape-growing regions such as Champagne, Bordeaux, and Burgundy are familiar to wine-lovers around the world. At the table, French wines are served alongside the many wonderful dishes for which French chefs are famous. Meals may include delicately flavored soups, seafoods such as mussels and lobsters, juicy steaks, delicious pastries, tasty fruits, and a variety of local cheeses. However, in some places these traditions are changing. More and more French families are eating convenience, or "fast" foods, and French wine exports are being challenged by wines from the Americas and Australia.

Tour de France

The Tour de France is the best-known cycle road race in the world, and the most grueling. Cyclists hunch over their ultra-light, multiple-geared machines as they climb steep roads into the mountains, or sweep in a pack through city streets. The roads are lined with millions of fans. The race was founded in 1903 and its route, which changes each year, varies in length from about 1,850 mi to 3,000 mi (3,000–5,000 km).

Peoples of France and Monaco

French

Monégasque

The French are of mixed Celtic, Germanic, and Italic descent. The French language is spoken throughout the country and in many other parts of the world which in the 1800s were part of the French Empire. Today French is still an important international language. Modern Celts include the Bretons of the Atlantic northwest, whose language is closely related to Welsh. Basques live in the Atlantic southwest and across the Spanish border. People of Italic or Mediterranean origin include the people of Monaco and Provence in the southeast, who speak a dialect of French, the Corsicans, and the Catalans of the southwest, whose homeland stretches across the Spanish border. The Alsatians are a Germanic people who live on France's eastern border. Many Arabs, Africans, and Asians from former colonies have settled in France.

Paris

Paris is one of the world's most beautiful and important cities, located on the banks and islands of the Seine River. Its landmarks include the vast medieval cathedral of Notre Dame, the hilly ridge of the old artists' district known as Montmartre, and the instantly recognized "iron needle" of the Eiffel Tower. The tower was designed by engineer Alexandre Gustave Eiffel (1832-1923) and is 900 ft (300 m)

high. It was completed in 1889 as part of the Paris Exposition (exhibition). Paris has broad, tree-lined avenues, grand arches and bridges, and fine old palaces. The city also boasts famous stores and restaurants, splendid opera houses, museums, and art galleries. Paris is the hub of the country's road and rail network and a powerful center of national government. It is by far the biggest city in France, with a population of more than 9 million.

Fast tracking

France's national rail company is called the SNCF *(Société Nationale des Chemins de Fer Français)*. It operates a modern, efficient system of railroads that links into the Trans-European network, connecting with the U.K. through a tunnel beneath the Channel. France is a world leader in the development of ultra-streamlined, high-speed trains, or TGVs *(Trains à Grande Vitesse)*.

Sunny crops

Yellow sunflowers brighten the landscape in the Aude valley, near Carcassone. In 1888, the great Dutch artist Vincent van Gogh (1853-90) painted flowers like these, when he lived at Arles in the southern French region of Provence. Sunflowers are native to Central America, but they have long been a common crop in France and other Mediterranean lands, such as Spain and the Balkans. Their large blooms ripen to form edible seeds that can be pressed to yield cooking oil. Other crops that thrive in the warm sunshine of southern France include rice (grown in the Camargue wetlands of the Rhône delta), olives, peaches, and melons. Fragrant lavender is grown in Provence for the perfume trade.

Monaco

The tiny principality of Monaco, on the Mediterranean coast, is a densely populated territory that includes land reclaimed from the sea. The economy depends on banking and finance and numerous international millionaires have made their homes here, mooring their gleaming luxury yachts in the harbor. Gamblers visit the famous casino at Monte Carlo. Each May the twisting streets are sealed off for the Formula One motor racing Grand Prix, a stern test of driving skills.

41

IBERIAN PENINSULA

In the southwest, the European mainland forms the broad peninsula of Iberia, with its long Atlantic and Mediterranean coastlines.

Iberia's northern coasts are mostly green and moist, but most of the region has hot, dry summers. At the center is a dry plateau fringed by the Cantabrian, Pyrenees, and Sierra Nevada mountains. Tucked away in the Pyrenees is Andorra, one of Europe's historic mini-states. The majority of its population makes a living from tourism and winter sports. The naval base of Gibraltar lies off the southern coast of Spain. This rocky outpost is an overseas territory of the U.K., although Spain disputes the situation.

Both Portugal and Spain grow citrus fruits and olives, and export wines, sherry, and port. With a recent history of rural poverty, both nations have benefited from joining the European Union (EU). Spain is rich in mineral resources and in industrial power, producing cars, textiles, and footwear. Many tourists visit from northern Europe. Mediterranean coasts in particular have many large and sometimes crowded holiday resorts.

Flamenco

Flamenco is the popular folk music of the Andalucia region, which surrounds the city of Seville in southern Spain. Dancers in colorful dresses step, stamp, and clap to powerful, soulful singing accompanied by energetically strummed acoustic guitars. Flamenco has been strongly influenced by the Romany or Gitano (Gypsy) tradition, and also by people who settled in medieval Spain, such as the Moors (from Morocco) and Jews. It has, in turn, influenced modern styles of European pop music.

The *corrida*

The *corrida* is the Spanish bullfight, which has a long history. Bulls specially bred for fighting are attacked with lances and barbed darts, and finally killed in the ring. The bullfighter, or matador, risks his life in the arena. To its critics, bullfighting is cruel and barbaric. To its aficionados (fans), it is an ancient and moving ritual.

Paella

The classic dish of southern Spain's Valencia region is paella, named after the heavy iron pan in which it is slowly simmered. It is made from local rice, flavored with saffron and garlic, and mixed with shrimp, mussels, or other shellfish, chicken, or diced meat. Each region of Spain has its own food specialties, such as lobster, tuna, sardines, ham, spicy sausages, hotpots, and beans, served with salads and vegetables bought fresh from the local market.

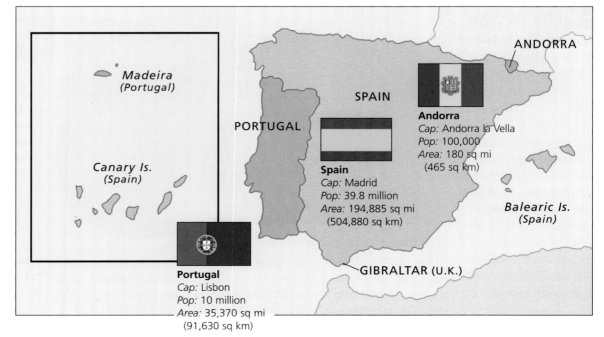

Madeira
(Portugal)

Canary Is.
(Spain)

PORTUGAL

SPAIN

ANDORRA

Andorra
Cap: Andorra la Vella
Pop: 100,000
Area: 180 sq mi
(465 sq km)

Spain
Cap: Madrid
Pop: 39.8 million
Area: 194,885 sq mi
(504,880 sq km)

Balearic Is.
(Spain)

Portugal
Cap: Lisbon
Pop: 10 million
Area: 35,370 sq mi
(91,630 sq km)

GIBRALTAR (U.K.)

Peoples of the Iberian peninsula

Spanish

Portuguese

Of mixed descent, the Spanish and Portuguese people have Iberian, Celtic, Greek, Italic, Germanic, and Moorish ancestors. The Spanish and Portuguese languages are spoken not just in Iberia, but also through most of Central and South America. Many other peoples in Spain have retained their own cultures and languages. The Catalans are a Mediterranean people who live around Barcelona and also in Andorra and the Balearic Islands. The Asturians and Galicians of the north have Celtic ancestry. The Basques of the northeast speak a tongue unrelated to any other European language. Many of them campaign, sometimes violently, to become independent from Spain. Other ethnic groups include the Romany (Gypsies) and more recent immigrants from Morocco to the south, who are of Arab or Berber descent.

Riding to the *Feria*

For an entire week each Apr l, the southern Spanish city of Seville is taken over by a fair called the *Feria de Abril*. By day, parades take place of carriages and horseback riders in traditional Andalucian costumes, demonstrating their great riding and driving skills. At night, there are parties and wild dancing in large public tents called *casetas*. A Roman Catholic country, Spain particularly loves historical pageants and colorful festivals of Christian worship. In Holy Week (before Easter Sunday) and on saints' days, statues and shrines are carried through villages and cities.

Knights and castles

Spain is famous for its castles, which date back to the Middle Ages. During this period, Christian knights tried to win back regions which had been taken from them by invading Moors. At the time, the Spanish city of Toledo was famous for making swords and armor. The writer Miguel de Cervantes (1547–1616) mocked the Spanish love of knighthood and chivalry. In his novel *Don Quixote*, the aging hero of that name lives in a fantasy world and charges at the windmills of La Mancha region, believing them to be enemy giants!

Moorish architecture

Villages of whitewashed houses cling to the rocky hillsides of southern Spain. They are very similar to the old dwellings of Morocco, which lies just 8 mi (13 km) to the south of Spain, across the Strait of Gibraltar. Between 711 and 1492, much of Spain was settled by Moors—Muslim Berbers and Arabs from North Africa. Moorish buildings survive today, such as the fabulous Alhambra palace in Granada.

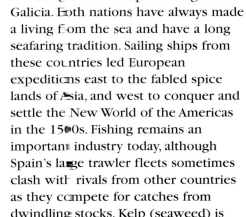

A living from the sea

Fishing harbors line the Atlantic coasts of Portugal and the Spanish region of Galicia. Both nations have always made a living from the sea and have a long seafaring tradition. Sailing ships from these countries led European expeditions east to the fabled spice lands of Asia, and west to conquer and settle the New World of the Americas in the 1500s. Fishing remains an important industry today, although Spain's large trawler fleets sometimes clash with rivals from other countries as they compete for catches from dwindling stocks. Kelp (seaweed) is harvested as fertilizer.

43

ITALY & MALTA

The boot-shaped Italian peninsula extends into the central Mediterranean Sea, flanked by the islands of Sardinia, Sicily, and Malta.

The northernmost parts of Italy occupy the southern slopes of the Alps Mountains, with their snowy peaks and blue lakes, and the broad fertile plains surrounding the Po River. The "backbone" of the region is the ridge of the Appennine mountains, which runs down the length of the Italian peninsula. Vineyards in the foothills drop to fertile coastal regions. Climate is generally warm and sunny, becoming hotter, drier, and more dusty to the southern tip. Italy is a founding member of the European Union (EU). Its northern cities are prosperous and fashionable, but many southerners are poor farmers. The tiny independent republic of San Marino lies entirely within Italy, as does the Vatican City, the international headquarters of the Catholic Church, in Rome. The islands of Malta, about 60 miles (96 km) south of Sicily, form another independent republic.

Squisito!

Delicious! Italian food, made with garlic, onions, mushrooms, tomatoes, and greens direct from the market, has become popular in many parts of the world. Many meals are based on pasta, which comes in all shapes and sizes, from spaghetti to macaroni. Rice can be cooked into a moist savory risotto or a sweet pudding. Many Italian dishes are flavored with herbs such as oregano or basil, or with cheeses such as Parmesan or ricotta. Parma is famous for its ham, and Venice for its seafoods, such as squid. Italy produces more wine than any other country in the world and its many ways of serving coffee have entered other languages as well as Italian. For example, espresso is a small cup of black, very strong coffee. Eating in Italy is entertainment for the whole family.

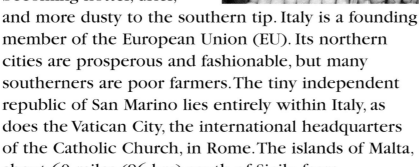

Venice

Northeastern Italy borders the Adriatic Sea, which forms a large, shallow lagoon dotted with small islands. At its center, Venice is one of the world's most beautiful cities. It is built around a network of canals, which offer quicker routes around the city, compared to the maze of narrow streets and alleys. Waterbuses called *vaporetti* provide transportation, but romantic tourists prefer the traditional hand-oared gondola. Venice was once an independent republic—a city-state which traded with countries as far away as China. It has magnificent cathedrals, palaces, squares, bridges, and treasured works of art—especially from the Renaissance period, which began in Italy.

San Marino
Cap: San Marino
Pop: 30,000
Area: 24 sq mi
(61 sq km)

Italy
Cap: Rome
Pop: 57.8 million
Area: 116,280 sq mi
(301,245 sq km)

Vatican City State
Pop: 1,000
Area: 0.17 sq mi
(0.4 sq km)

Malta
Cap: Valletta
Pop: 400,000
Area: 122 sq mi
(316 sq km)

ITALY
CORSICA (France)
SAN MARINO
VATICAN CITY STATE
SARDINIA
SICILY
MALTA

Peoples of Italy and Malta

Italian

Maltese

Italians make up the great majority of the population in Italy, although there are many variants in dialects, customs, and ways of life. This variety is evident especially among the Sicilians and the Sards of Sardinia. Some people are descended from ancient Italian tribes, such as the Etruscans, while others have ancestors among later settlers, such as Greeks, Normans, and, in the northwest, Lombards. They all speak Italian, an Italic language which grew out of ancient Latin. The Eastern Ladins of the Dolomite range are an Alpine people whose language is related to that of the Romansh speakers in Switzerland. There is a small Slavic community near the Slovenian border to the east. The Maltese people are of mixed Italian, Spanish, Arab, Norman, and Sicilian origin, and these influences are reflected in their unique language.

The "Eternal City"

The Colosseum was built by the ancient Romans in 72–80 A.D. and its ruins stand at the center of Rome, Italy's capital on the Tiber River. Crowds roared as combatants called gladiators fought to the death in the blood-soaked arena. Even 2,000 years ago, Rome was a city of about 1 million people, and the center of a huge empire. The rule of Rome came to an end when the city was sacked by Germanic invaders in 476 A.D. In the Middle Ages, Rome became the center of the Catholic Church. Modern Rome is a lively city with a population of over 3 million and many historic sites.

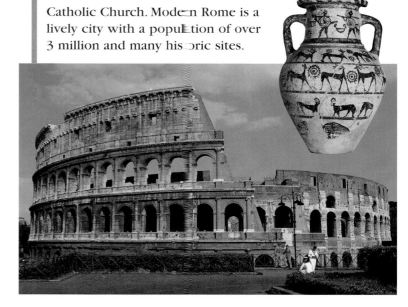

Blue seas

Warm Italian and Maltese tourist resorts attract visitors, especially from northern Europe. The Mediterranean divides around Italy into the Tyrrhenian and Adriatic Seas. But the shallow waters have suffered industrial pollution.

The smart set

Designer stores line the streets in many Italian cities. The nation is known for its skills in fashion, graphics, and industrial design, producing household goods, computers, plastics, smart leather bags, coats, and shoes. Milan is a world center of the fashion industry. Well-known makes of family car, such as Fiat, are Italian. The country also has a long history of designing and racing fast cars, with Ferrari as a leading name.

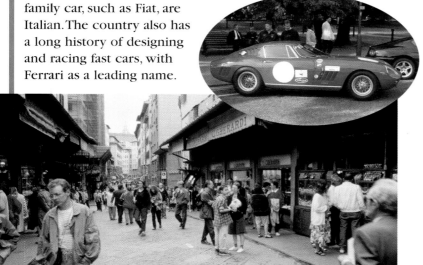

Pisa's leaning tower

The city of Pisa, in the northern Italian region of Tuscany, has a cathedral with a fine medieval bell tower which is 178.8 ft (54.5 m) tall. Even as it was being built during the 1200s and 1300s, it began to lean over as its foundations shifted. By the 1980s, the tower was in danger of toppling. Engineering work to prop it up took 12 years and was completed in 2001. The tower is still tilted, but it is safe and can be visited by tourists.

Farmers

Italy's fertile lowland regions, such as Campania around Naples, have been farmed for thousands of years. Fifty years ago, most

Italians still worked the land. Today, however, economic changes and the increased use of agricultural machinery mean that farmers make up only 7 percent of the work force. Many Italian crops are particularly well suited to the hot, Mediterranean climate—especially olives (pressed to make olive oil), as well as rice, tomatoes, oranges, lemons and other citrus fruits, and grapes for wine. Grain crops include corn, wheat, barley and oats.

From the high peaks and glaciers of the Alps, the land drops to the forests and hills of southern Germany.

Farther north, heathland gives way to a wide northern plain and the sandy North Sea and Baltic coasts. Germany, a leading member of the EU, has the Oder River to the east and the Rhine and Moselle rivers to the west. Its historic towns date back to the Middle Ages, and large modern cities make it a world leader in industry and finance. Exports include cars, chemicals, electrical goods, and optical instruments.

The mountains and lakes of Switzerland, Liechtenstein, and Austria attract many tourists. Switzerland, noted for its watches and dairy products, is the center of international institutions such as the World Health Organization. Austria once ruled a large Central European empire and today produces timber, paper, machinery, and glass.

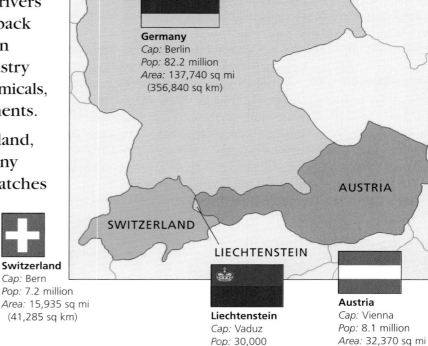

GERMANY

Germany
Cap: Berlin
Pop: 82.2 million
Area: 137,740 sq mi
(356,840 sq km)

AUSTRIA

SWITZERLAND

LIECHTENSTEIN

Switzerland
Cap: Bern
Pop: 7.2 million
Area: 15,935 sq mi
(41,285 sq km)

Liechtenstein
Cap: Vaduz
Pop: 30,000
Area: 62 sq mi
(160 sq km)

Austria
Cap: Vienna
Pop: 8.1 million
Area: 32,370 sq mi
(83,855 sq km)

German journeys

Visitors to Germany are attracted to the lively capital Berlin, picturesque southern regions like the Black Forest, and Munich's famous beer festival. Highway and rail networks link the regions and much industrial freight travels by barge along waterways. A major transit route is the Rhine, from Switzerland through Germany to the Netherlands and the North Sea.

Lands of music

Salzburg, in Austria, is a historical city with a fine cathedral and castle. It was the birthplace of the great composer Wolfgang Amadeus Mozart (1756-91). A music festival in his memory is held in the city each year. The Austrian capital, Vienna, is associated with a ballroom dance called the waltz, made popular by Johann Strauss (1804-49) and his son Johann Strauss the Younger (1825-99). Germany, too, has played an extraordinary part in the history and development of classical music. Its composers include Johann Bach (1685-1750), Ludwig van Beethoven (1770-1827), Johannes Brahms (1833-97), and Richard Wagner (1813-83).

Peoples of Germany and the Alps

German

Austrian

The Germans are a mainly Germanic people who are related to the English, Dutch, and Scandinavians. The German language is spoken throughout Germany. Its official version is known as High German, but there are also many regional dialects. Slavic peoples in Germany include the Sorbs or Wends and various immigrants from Eastern Europe. Turks have also settled in many German cities. In addition, German-speakers live in Austria, Liechtenstein, and northern and central Switzerland, where Swiss-German has become a language in its own right. Peoples from neighboring lands overlap Switzerland's other borders. In the west and southwest are Swiss-French. In the southern valleys of the Alps are Swiss-Italians and Western Ladins, who speak a language called Romansh. French, Italian, and Romansh are all Italic, or Romance, languages.

Living in the Alps

Between the Alpine peaks, villages and towns occupy the valley floors, which are green in summer and snowy in winter. Houses are often constructed in the chalet style—timber-built with wide, sloping roofs to shed the snow. Herds of cattle, goats, and sheep are led up to high mountain pastures in the summer, when the thaw allows them to graze on the fresh grass. Many mountain festivals celebrate alpine folk dancing, the music of the gigantic alphorn, and a type of high-pitched, fast-paced singing known as yodeling.

Alpine sports

The Alps have many popular ski resorts. In these mountains, various alpine sports were first developed, such as bobsledding in the 1880s. It was here, too, that mountaineering and rock climbing first became a pastime, carried out for pleasure rather than necessity.

Eating well

Germany is well known for its sausages and cold meats, dark rye breads, white wines, and flavorful beers. Switzerland is the land of cheeses, such as Emmenthal and Gruyère, and melted cheese forms the basis of many Swiss dishes. Delicious cakes and tarts are served with coffee in the famous cafés of Vienna, Austria.

Winter masks

In Germany and Austria, carnival is called *Fasching* or *Fastnacht*. In the Tyrol region of Austria, many carnival customs date back to pre-Christian times. Masks are worn, with some intended to scare and cause fear—looking like bears or devils—while others are elegant and beautiful. The tall headdresses worn at Imst are decorated with artificial flowers, tinsel, glass, and mirrors.

Liechtenstein

Tiny Liechtenstein's population is similar to that of an average town. It is a relic of history, but in modern times it has become very wealthy as a result of tourism, banking, finance, and its particular taxation laws. Liechtenstein lies on the Rhine River, between Switzerland and Austria. It has close links with Switzerland and shares the same currency.

BALKAN PENINSULA

EUROPE

The Balkan peninsula is bordered by the Adriatic and Ionian Seas in the west, and by the Aegean and Black Seas in the east.

Until 1991, the western Balkans were occupied by the large country of Yugoslavia. Now four of its former provinces are independent countries—Slovenia, Croatia, Bosnia-Herzegovina, and Macedonia. Yugoslavia now contains only the provinces of Serbia, Kosovo, and Montenegro. All these lands are rocky, with cold winters inland, but hot summers. The eastern Balkans include two larger countries of Romania and Bulgaria, which flank the Danube River. They have fertile plains and forested mountain slopes. The southern Balkans taper to form Albania, one of Europe's poorest countries, and Greece, which is wealthier and a member of the EU. Both have ragged coasts of headlands and islands.

Kazanluk parade

Folk costumes are worn for a festival at Kazanluk, a central Bulgarian city on the southern rim of the Balkan mountain range. Kazanluk lies in a district famed for roses, which are processed into scented oils for the perfume industry. Other crops include tobacco and grapes for wine-making. All the Balkan countries except Greece had communist governments, with state-owned industries, until 1990–91. They are now moving toward an economic system like that of Western Europe.

Seeking refuge

Many Albanians, seeking to escape the poverty of their homeland, have fled to Greece and Italy. Romany (Gypsies) from Romania have also been on the move westward, in search of a generally higher standard of living. Many poor people were uprooted in the former lands of Yugoslavia, which were devastated by wars and ethnic conflict during the 1990s. The western Balkans desperately need peace and time to rebuild as nations.

Slovenia
Cap: Ljubljana
Pop: 2 million
Area: 7,815 sq mi
(20,250 sq km)

Croatia
Cap: Zagreb
Pop: 4.7 million
Area: 21,825 sq mi
(56,540 sq km)

Romania
Cap: Bucharest
Pop: 22.4 million
Area: 91,675 sq mi
(237,500 sq km)

Bosnia-Herzegovina
Cap: Sarajevo
Pop: 3.4 million
Area: 19,735 sq mi
(51,130 sq km)

Yugoslavia (Serbia-Montenegro)
Cap: Belgrade
Pop: 10.7 million
Area: 39,435 sq mi
(102,170 sq km)

Macedonia (Former Yugoslav Republic)
Cap: Skopje
Pop: 2 million
Area: 9,925 sq mi
(25,715 sq km)

Bulgaria
Cap: Sofia
Pop: 8.1 million
Area: 42,810 sq mi
(110,910 sq km)

Albania
Cap: Tiranë
Pop: 3.4 million
Area: 11,100 sq mi
(28,750 sq km)

Greece
Cap: Athens
Pop: 10.9 million
Area: 50,945 sq mi
(131,985 sq km)

SLOVENIA

CROATIA

ROMANIA

BOSNIA-HERZEGOVINA

YUGOSLAVIA

BULGARIA

FYR MACEDONIA

ALBANIA

GREECE

Peoples of the Balkan peninsula

Bosnian

Romanian

The Slovenians, Croatians, Bosnians, Serbs, Montenegrins, and many Macedonians living in the Former Yugoslav Republic are all Slavic peoples, speaking similar but distinct languages. Bitter regional divisions also involve religious conflict between Muslims and Christians. There are large populations of Romany (Gypsy) throughout the region. The Romanians and Bulgarians are both of mixed origin. Romanians are partly Slavic and partly the descendants of the Dacians of the Roman Empire. Bulgarians are also partly Slavic but also descended from the Bulgars, a Turkic people. The Albanians are an ancient Balkan people living in Albania, Montenegro, and Kosovo. The Greeks live throughout mainland Greece and the islands, with cultures varying greatly between Greek Macedonia in the north and Crete in the Eastern Mediterranean to the south.

Salt farming in Slovenia

Seawater is collected in reservoirs and then dried off, leaving behind glistening sea or rock salt. This can be collected for industrial use or purified for cooking. Slovenia is the most westerly nation in the Balkans, and tends to look westward to its Alpine neighbors, with their more liberal market-force economies, rather than eastward to Croatia. Slovenia is a land of forested mountains and limestone caves, with a small coastline on the Gulf of Trieste. It is the only part of the former Yugoslavia to have avoided serious conflict in recent

years. One reason for this is that Slovenes make up over 90 percent of the population, so there have not been bitter ethnic divisions as in neighboring states. The years of peace have helped to stabilize and safeguard the economy, which is based on tourism, steel-making, chemicals, paper, and textiles. Slovenia is wealthier than any other former Yugoslav nation.

Gateway to Greece

Many of the ferries traveling from one Greek island to another finally anchor in Piraeus, the port for Athens. The Greeks have been seafarers for more than 2,000 years and shipping remains an important part of their economy. Greece exports produce such as goat's cheeses and yogurt, olives, honey, and melons. Much of the land is rocky and dry, unsuitable for farming. There are large industrial areas around Piraeus and Thessaloniki in the north. Pretty villages with old Greek Orthodox churches, sunshine, and warm seas have made Greece one of the world's most popular tourist destinations.

Souvláki

Skewered lamb grilled over charcoal is called *souvláki*. Popular Greek dishes include stuffed vineleaves and peppers and *moussaka* (an eggplant casserole). The Greek wine *retsina* takes on the taste of pine resin from its storage casks.

Ancient Greeks

Europe's first great civilizations developed in Greece, and many ancient archeological sites still survive today. Crete was the site of fabulous Minoan royal palaces 4,000 years ago. The classical age of Greece began about 2,500 years ago, producing impressive temples, theaters, statues, and, in Athens, the world's first attempts at democratic government.

Romania

A statue of the Russian revolutionary leader Lenin (1870-1924) lies toppled in Bucharest, capital of Romania. This nation had communist governments until 1989, by which time it had fallen out with the Soviet Union and become a type of family dictatorship. Romania lies on the eastern fringe of Europe. Remote and forested, its Carpathian Mountains form twin ranges in the interior, with the Danube River along the southern frontier, its delta emptying into the Black Sea. Major crops are wheat, corn, sunflowers, beets, and grapes.

CENTRAL & BALTIC

EUROPE

A wide plain stretches across Poland. To the north are the sandy shores of the Baltic states. Southward lie the mountains and forests of Europe's heartland.

The political map of Central Europe and the eastern Baltic has changed numerous times. Estonia, Latvia, and Lithuania became independent from the Soviet Union (now the Russian Federation) in 1991. They export foodstuffs, timber, textiles, and machinery. Poland, which has historical links with Lithuania, is a huge land of farms and forests, fine old cities, industrial centers, and coalfields. The land rises to the Sudeten and Tatra mountains along its southern borders. The Czech Republic, with wooded hills and river valleys, produces beers and glassware. Until 1993, it was one nation with its mountainous neighbor, Slovakia. In Hungary the mountains descend to rolling plains and farmland.

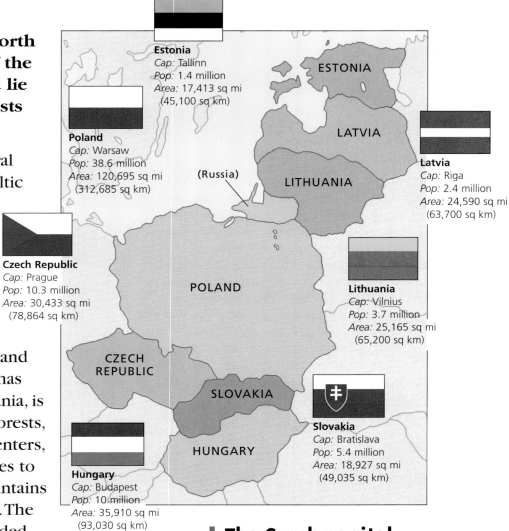

Estonia
Cap: Tallinn
Pop: 1.4 million
Area: 17,413 sq mi
(45,100 sq km)

Poland
Cap: Warsaw
Pop: 38.6 million
Area: 120,695 sq mi
(312,685 sq km)

Latvia
Cap: Riga
Pop: 2.4 million
Area: 24,590 sq mi
(63,700 sq km)

Czech Republic
Cap: Prague
Pop: 10.3 million
Area: 30,433 sq mi
(78,864 sq km)

Lithuania
Cap: Vilnius
Pop: 3.7 million
Area: 25,165 sq mi
(65,200 sq km)

Slovakia
Cap: Bratislava
Pop: 5.4 million
Area: 18,927 sq mi
(49,035 sq km)

Hungary
Cap: Budapest
Pop: 10 million
Area: 35,910 sq mi
(93,030 sq km)

(Russia)

The Czech capital

Prague, in the Czech region of Bohemia, was already one of Europe's great centers in the Middle Ages, when it had many German inhabitants. The city was built beside the Vltava River and has many beautiful old bridges, churches, and squares, including the famous Wenceslas Square. Prague is a center of the arts, book publishing, and learning, but also an industrial powerhouse producing chemicals, paper, and machines. It is a lively capital that has become quite popular with tourists.

Costumes and festivals

The medieval kingdom of Bohemia was famous for its music and merrymaking. The modern Czech republic occupies part of the former Bohemia and its people enjoy all kinds of music, too. Local men and women dress in traditional costumes to perform dances at folk festivals. In many parts of Central Europe, and especially in the Baltic states, costume and music were a way of expressing national identity during long years of domination by the Soviet Union, from 1945 until 1990.

Peoples of Central Europe and the Baltic

Hungarian

Latvian

The Czechs, Poles, and Slovaks are all Slavic peoples. So, too, are the many Russians who live in the Baltic states and the Boyks, Lemks, Belarussians, and Ukrainians who form minorities in Poland. There is also a German minority in Poland, mostly living in the coal-mining regions of Silesia. The Balts include the Lithuanians and the Latvians. The Estonians and Livs (a small minority living in Latvia) belong to the family of Finno-Ugric speakers. They are distant cousins of the Magyars of Hungary, who invaded the Hungarian Plain about 1,200 years ago. Their descendants make up 90 percent of the Hungarian population. Central Europe has a large number of Romany and Sinte, the traveling people known more commonly as Gypsies. This group of people has been persecuted for its way of life over many years.

Industrial age

The Baltic states have extensive forests and peat bogs, which are wetlands with a fibrous soil made up of ancient, semi-rotted plant remains. Timber is exported or pulped to make paper. Peat can be excavated, to burn as a fuel or be used as a compost. The rich resources of Poland and Central Europe include timber, coal, sulfur, copper, offshore oil, natural gas, lead, silver, and salt. Industry in many regions was developed rapidly under communist rule, during the 1950s. In the rush to build factories, mills and mines, the environment often suffered severe damage. Serious air pollution was caused by steelworks and factories in Poland and by the burning of fuels made from oil shale in Estonia. These created ongoing health problems for people living near industrial centers, and many regions are still struggling with pollution today.

Budapest

Budapest, Hungary's capital, grew from two towns, Buda and Pest, built on the banks of the Danube River, Europe's second longest river. The bustling city is the center of national government and has a population of more than 2 million people. Its attractions include many historical churches and old universities, as well as more recent industrial suburbs. Factories process fruits, grains, and other crops grown on the wide, rolling Hungarian Plain.

Resistance

This memorial in Warsaw, Poland's capital on the Vistula River, honors those who died in the city's uprisings of 1943 and 1944. As long ago as the 1700s, Poland became dominated by its powerful neighbors—Swedes, Germans, and Russians took turns to invade and control the region. The German Nazis again invaded Poland in 1939, marking the start of World War II. Under German rule, millions of Polish Jews, Romany, and Slavs in Warsaw, and all across Poland, were herded together into ghettos or murdered. In 1944, the Jews, who were in immediate danger of being exterminated by the German occupiers, rebelled against the German rule in the Warsaw Uprising. After the war, the Soviet Union (U.S.S.R.) tried to control the way in which Poland was governed. In 1989, the Poles at last gained real freedom.

Sounds of the zither

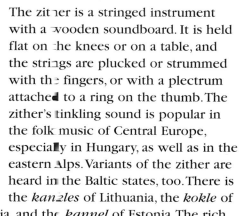

The zither is a stringed instrument with a wooden soundboard. It is held flat on the knees or on a table, and the strings are plucked or strummed with the fingers, or with a plectrum attached to a ring on the thumb. The zither's tinkling sound is popular in the folk music of Central Europe, especially in Hungary, as well as in the eastern Alps. Variants of the zither are heard in the Baltic states, too. There is the *kanzles* of Lithuania, the *kokle* of Latvia, and the *kannel* of Estonia. The rich folk music of Central Europe and the Baltic states, with traditions of wandering minstrels and storytellers, has inspired many great classical composers.

EUROPE

The mountain ranges of the Urals and the Caucasus form the continental border between Europe and Asia. The vast Russian nation straddles the two continents.

The Russian Federation is by far the biggest country on Earth. It extends from the Arctic Ocean in the north, through conifer forests to the southern steppes (grasslands), deserts, and mountains. Russia also includes the vast wilderness of Siberia, which stretches north and east across Asia to the Pacific Ocean.

Russia has many natural resources—coal, oil, natural gas, nickel, and copper. It grows huge amounts of wheat, sugar beets, potatoes, and fruits, and its forests provide timber. Most Russians live to the west of the Ural Mountains in European Russia, where there are numerous cities and factories.

From 1922 until 1991, Russia was part of an even larger nation called the Soviet Union (U.S.S.R.). Ruled by a communist government, all of its industries were owned by the state. The U.S.S.R. split in 1991. Russia is now moving toward an economy of private businesses and market forces, like those of Western European countries.

Other parts of the U.S.S.R. are now independent nations producing machinery, iron, steel, and wheat. Belarus, Ukraine, and Moldova lie to the west of Russia, while Georgia lies to the south, in the Caucasus Mountains.

Moscow life

The Russian capital of Moscow is built around a river of the same name. The climate of the capital is bitterly cold and snowy in winter, but it can be warm in summer. Moscow's historical center is an imposing red-walled fort named the Kremlin, used as the government's headquarters. The city has many large official buildings, offices, apartment blocks, and hotels that date from the Soviet period. The GUM building was a state-owned department store during that time, but it is now a mall of private stores selling luxury goods to Muscovites (Moscow-dwellers). The subway, or Metro, has 150 stations. Many are decorated in the ornate style of the 1930s.

Belarus
Cap: Minsk
Pop: 10 million
Area: 80,290 sq mi
(208,000 sq km)

Ukraine
Cap: Kiev
Pop: 49.1 million
Area: 233,030 sq mi
(603,700 sq km)

Moldova
Cap: Chisinau
Pop: 4.3 million
Area: 13,010 sq mi
(33,700 sq km)

Russian Federation
Cap: Moscow
Pop: 144.4 million
Area: 6,592,110 sq mi
(17,078,005 sq km)

Georgia
Cap: Tbilisi
Pop: 5.5 million
Area: 26,905 sq mi
(69,700 sq km)

Peoples of Russia and Eastern Europe

Belarussian

Russian

Slavic peoples include the Belarussians, the Ukrainians, and the Russians, each of which has its own language, although the three languages are closely related. Originating from Eastern Europe, the Russians have also settled in much of Siberia. They make up 80 percent of the population within the Russian Federation. Many Slavs also live in Moldova, although most Moldovans are actually relatives of the Romanians. The Georgians are a Caucasian people, as are the Chechens to their northeast, many of whom are currently fighting for their own state, independent of Russia. Peoples native to Arctic Russia include the Nentsi or Samoyeds, who are related to the Saami of Scandinavia, the Komi, and the Chukchi, relatives of the North American Inuit. Siberian peoples include the Yakuts and Evenks. The Tatars and the Buryats share Mongol origins.

Easter eggs

Many Slavic countries have a tradition of painting eggs with colorful designs for the Christian festival of Easter Sunday. Called *pysanky*, egg-painting is far more than a custom—it is a skilled art. In Russia, egg-decoration achieved worldwide fame due to the designer Peter Carl Fabergé (1846-1920). Fabergé created ornate eggs for the royal family, made from gold, silver, and jewels. Today, they are prized as priceless works of art.

Trans-Siberian railroad

The world's longest rail network links Yaroslavsky station, Moscow, with the Pacific port of Vladivostok far to the east. Lines branch south through Mongolia and China (Manchuria) to Beijing. The main line is 5,803 mi (9,289 km) long. It crosses eight time zones, but clocks on the train stay on Moscow time. The journey lasts nearly a week. Despite heavy snowfalls, the service is amazingly punctual.

Icons and domes

In 988, the Slavs adopted the Christian faith in the city of Kiev. They followed the form of worship practiced in Byzantium and now known as the Eastern Orthodox Church. The powers of the church were limited during the Soviet period and its buildings neglected. Today, Russian churches are undergoing careful restoration. Many, like St. Basil's Cathedral in Moscow, have beautiful domes. Some also contain religious pictures called icons, which have been painted by monks since the Middle Ages, as acts of worship.

Ballet stars

Positioned on the Neva River, the beautiful city of St. Petersburg (formerly Leningrad) was once the capital of Russia. From 1738, it played a leading role in the history of ballet—it was here that *Sleeping Beauty* and *The Nutcracker* were first performed, both composed by Piotr Tchaikovsky (1840-93). The city's leading theater, the Mariinsky, is the home of the world-famous Kirov Ballet Company. Many of the greatest ballet and classical dancers of the last hundred years were trained here.

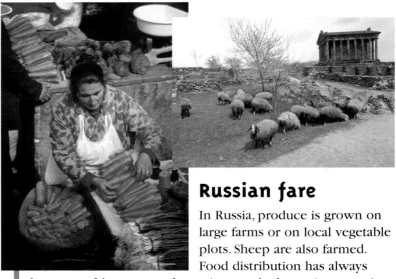

Russian fare

In Russia, produce is grown on large farms or on local vegetable plots. Sheep are also farmed. Food distribution has always been a problem across the nation, partly due to its great size. Shortages are still common, and today many people gather wild mushrooms and berries in forests, or fish in the lakes and rivers. Russian cooking often makes use of potatoes and cabbage. Meals include *borscht* (beetroot soup), pancakes and dumplings, pickles, or beef Stroganoff. Caviar is an expensive delicacy made from the eggs of a large fish called the sturgeon, which is becoming increasingly rare.

ASIA

Asia is the world's biggest continent, forming the main part of the Eurasian land mass. In the west it is separated from Europe by the Ural and Caucasus mountain ranges and the Mediterranean and Black seas. Its other shores are on the Arctic, Pacific, and Indian Oceans. Asian landscapes vary from the ice and snow of the Arctic tundra and northern conifer forests, to windy mountains and steppes, vast plains of scrub and desert, dense tropical rain forests, swamps, and steamy coastal wetlands.

Many advanced civilizations developed in Asia in ancient times. The continent saw the invention of the wheel, the taming of the horse, and the first writing. Asia was also the birthplace of several great religions, including Hinduism, Buddhism, Judaism, Christianity, and Islam. Modern Asia is a large land of crowded cities and empty wildernesses. It is a land where a few people are very wealthy but the majority of people are desperately poor.

The crowded continent

Asia has a population of 3.7 billion, which is almost two-thirds of all the people living in the world today. China and India alone, the planet's two most populous nations, have a population of more than 2.3 billion people. Growth is so rapid that by the year 2050, the Asian total is expected to reach a figure of 5.2 billion. Asia has some of the most densely populated areas on Earth, not just in massive cities such as Tokyo in Japan and Macao in China, but also across whole countries, like Bangladesh. Yet central and northern Asia are almost empty.

Village life

For thousands of years, people have occupied the fertile plains and valleys of Asia, such as those surrounding the Indus, Ganges, Huang, and Mekong rivers. They have sown and harvested crops, built villages, collected reeds, and survived both flood and famine. Mohandas Gandhi (1869–1948), who led the campaign to end British rule in India, believed that all people could learn from the simple practical activities of Asian village life.

Feeding the people

The most pressing problems facing many Asian governments are population increase and food—the growth, distribution, and sale of enough food for so many hungry mouths. Rice is the chief crop in Asia's most populated regions. Wild rice grows in wetlands and river valleys, but the many varieties of cultivated rice have to be grown in flooded paddy fields. These stretch across the landscape of southern China and Southeast Asia. In upland areas the fields take the form of irrigated level strips called terraces, excavated from the hillsides. Grain crops such as corn, wheat, and barley form a staple (basic) diet in other parts of Asia.

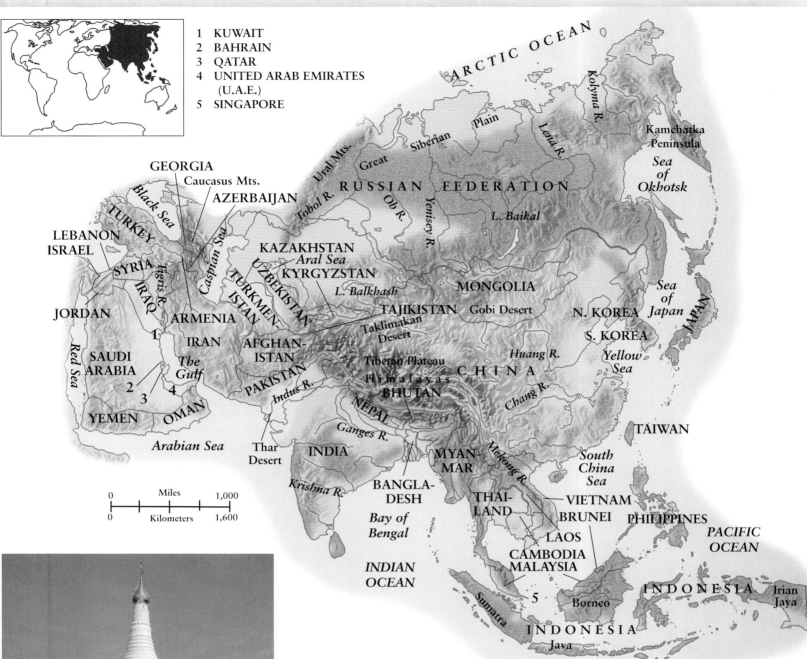

1 KUWAIT
2 BAHRAIN
3 QATAR
4 UNITED ARAB EMIRATES
  (U.A.E.)
5 SINGAPORE

ARCTIC OCEAN

Kolyma R.

Siberian Plain

Kamchatka Peninsula

Sea of Okhotsk

Ural Mts.

GEORGIA

Caucasus Mts.

AZERBAIJAN

Tobol R.

Ob R.

Yenisey R.

RUSSIAN FEDERATION

L. Baikal

TURKEY

Black Sea

LEBANON
ISRAEL

SYRIA

Caspian Sea

KAZAKHSTAN

Aral Sea

KYRGYZSTAN

MONGOLIA

Sea of Japan

Tigris R.

IRAQ

JORDAN

ARMENIA

TURKMEN-
ISTAN

UZBEKISTAN

L. Balkhash

TAJIKISTAN

Gobi Desert

N. KOREA

JAPAN

IRAN

AFGHAN-
ISTAN

Taklimakan
Desert

Huang R.

S. KOREA

Yellow
Sea

SAUDI
ARABIA

Red Sea

1

The
Gulf

PAKISTAN

Tibetan Plateau

CHINA

Himalayas

BHUTAN

Chang R.

2 3 4

Indus R.

NEPAL

TAIWAN

YEMEN

OMAN

Arabian Sea

Ganges R.

Thar
Desert

INDIA

MYAN-
MAR

Mekong R.

South
China
Sea

Krishna R.

BANGLA-
DESH

Bay of
Bengal

THAI-
LAND

VIETNAM

BRUNEI

PHILIPPINES

PACIFIC
OCEAN

INDIAN
OCEAN

LAOS

CAMBODIA
MALAYSIA

5

Borneo

INDONESIA

Irian
Jaya

Sumatra

INDONESIA

Java

Miles
0   1,000
0   1,600
Kilometers

Temples of Pagan

A stupa, or Buddhist shrine, points to the sky at the town of Pagan, Myanmar (formerly Burma). A thousand or more temples and shrines were built here between about 1050 and 1299. Gautama Buddha (c.563–483 B.C.) was a Nepalese prince who gave up his riches in order to preach about life, suffering, and happiness. His teachings are widely followed in many parts of Asia.

Mining and drilling

Datong in northern China is a center of coal-mining. Asia's most valued mineral resource is petroleum oil, produced from the Caspian Sea to Saudi Arabia in the west, and from Brunei to the South China Sea in the east. The vast northern region of Siberia is rich in metal ores such as iron, nickel, and copper.

THE NEAR EAST

ASIA

As travelers cross the Bosphorus in Turkey from Europe, they enter Asia. The nations of the Near East face the Mediterranean Sea.

The Anatolian peninsula, with the ancient name of Asia Minor, lies between the Black Sea and the eastern Mediterranean Sea. It is occupied by Turkey, the largest country of the region. The coastal climate is mild, but the inland plateaus, plains, and mountains are dry and dusty, with hot summers and cold winters. Turkey produces wheat, barley, tobacco, cotton, and fruit. Its Mediterranean beaches attract many tourists. The island of Cyprus shares the same warm climate.

Syria, Lebanon, and Israel border the Mediterranean's eastern end, with lands ideal for growing crops such as melons, oranges, and grapefruit. Inland, the terrain turns arid and is grazed by sheep and goats. In Syria, Jordan, and southern Israel are hot, sandy deserts.

The Near East has seen much turmoil. When the state of Israel was established in 1948, many Palestinians were displaced and became refugees, leading to wars, acts of terrorism, and military reprisals, which continued in spite of many efforts to find a peaceful solution.

City of many names

Istanbul is a beautiful Turkish city on the hilly European shore around an inlet called the Golden Horn, in the Bosphorus (the strait between the Mediterranean and Black Seas). In ancient times, it was known as Byzantium or Constantinople. In 330 A.D., it became the capital of the eastern Roman Empire, which later developed into the Christian Byzantine Empire. The empire finally fell to the Muslim Turks in 1453 and the city was the Turkish Ottoman Empire's capital. The Ottomans ruled most of the Near East and Balkans until 1920.

In Lebanon

A sect of Christians called Maronites make up a quarter of the Lebanese population. Their influence can be seen in the many Christian churches of the area, like this one just south of Beirut. Although the majority of Lebanese are Muslim, the Maronites ruled the country for years, leading to civil war in the 1970s–80s. Conflict between Israel and Palestinian Arabs also spilled into Lebanon. This beautiful land is being rebuilt in hope of a peaceful future.

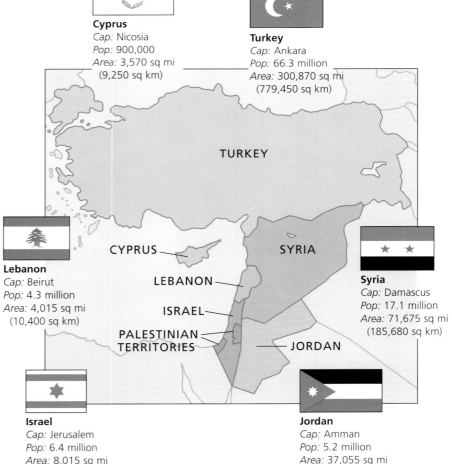

Cyprus
Cap: Nicosia
Pop: 900,000
Area: 3,570 sq mi
(9,250 sq km)

Turkey
Cap: Ankara
Pop: 66.3 million
Area: 300,870 sq mi
(779,450 sq km)

Lebanon
Cap: Beirut
Pop: 4.3 million
Area: 4,015 sq mi
(10,400 sq km)

Syria
Cap: Damascus
Pop: 17.1 million
Area: 71,675 sq mi
(185,680 sq km)

Israel
Cap: Jerusalem
Pop: 6.4 million
Area: 8,015 sq mi
(20,770 sq km)

Jordan
Cap: Amman
Pop: 5.2 million
Area: 37,055 sq mi
(96,000 sq km)

Peoples of the Near East

Jewish

Muslim

Languages of the Near East include Turkish, Greek, Kurdish, Hebrew, and Arabic. A people of Central Asian origin, the Turks make up 80 percent of the population in Turkey and 18 percent in Cyprus, where the majority of the people are Greek. Eastern Turkey lies within the traditional homelands of the Kurds, a people related to the Iranians. Many Kurds campaign to create an independent Kurdish nation, and this has resulted in political unrest and occasional violence. Various groups of Arabs live in Syria, Lebanon, Israel, the Palestinian Territories, and Jordan. Israel is a modern state founded in 1948 as a homeland for Jews, who occupied the region in biblical times. Scattered for nearly 2,000 years and often persecuted, they began returning to the region in the early 20th century.

Ephesus

With its wealth of ancient remains, Turkey is a rich hunting ground for historians and archaeologists. It is the site of the Stone Age town of Çatal Hüyük, which dates back to about 6250 B.C., and of the legendary city of Troy. The ruins of the ancient city of Ephesus, founded by the Greeks, still stand to the south of Izmir. Ephesus was a very wealthy city, famed for its great temple which was dedicated to the goddess Artemis (also known as Diana). The city was captured by the Macedonian Alexander the Great in 333 B.C. and by the Romans in 133 B.C. Ancient sites like these, coupled with hot sun and long coastlines, attract many tourists.

Buying food

Markets offer spices, almonds, dates, lemons, tomatoes, and peppers. Chickpeas are ground into a paste with garlic, or made into balls called *felafel*. Chicken and lamb, or fish along the coasts, can be grilled on skewers and served between pita bread as kebabs. Sweets include halva, made from honey and sesame paste. Small cups of Turkish coffee are black, strong, and sweet.

Jerusalem

Muslims (followers of Islam) believe that the Prophet Muhammad rode up to heaven from the Dome of the Rock, which is in the city of Jerusalem. In the old city are holy sites of three world faiths —Judaism, Christianity, and Islam. Jerusalem spreads across the eastern slopes of the Judaean hills, a region at risk from earthquakes. It is home to over half a million people. In 1948, Jerusalem was divided between Israel and Jordan. But after an armed conflict in 1967, called the Six Day War, Israel gained control of the whole city. Violent attacks continue in this historic yet troubled place.

Succot

The Jewish festival Chag Ha Succot (Feast of Tabernacles) is held each fall. For the festival, families build shelters roofed with freshly gathered branches and leaves outside their homes. Here, they eat their meals and sometimes sleep for seven days. Each shelter, called a Succah, is designed to remind the Jews that they once had to live in flimsy shelters while wandering through the harsh desert lands. During this period in the wilderness they were kept alive only by the mercy of God.

A desert city

The buildings of the ruined city of Petra, in Jordan, were carved from the rock of desert ravines. An Arabic people called the Nabataeans founded the city about 2,400 years ago. Five hundred years later, Petra was under Roman rule. Lying on the route to southern Asia, the city came to control the spice trade. It was later abandoned to the sand and wind. It has now been excavated and is visited by many tourists from around the world.

CENTRAL ASIA

Central Asia lies to the south of Russia. The Caucasus Mountains rise in the west, the Hindu Kush and Pamir in the east.

Much of Central Asia's landscape is very harsh and sparsely populated. Its habitats range from rocky wilderness and towering mountains, to steppes where sheep and goats graze the thin, dusty pasture. Droughts are common across the region, and the deserts can be scorching hot or bitterly cold. Central Asia is far from any ocean, yet it has several large inland waters. These include the world's biggest lake, the Caspian Sea, and the Aral Sea. The Aral was once also a vast lake, but it has rapidly shrunk by half its area, its waters diverted for crop irrigation.

The lands bordering the Russian Federation were part of the Soviet Union until 1991. Like Russia itself, their economies are moving from communist state control toward capitalist private ownership. Regional industries include oil and gas, textiles, wool, cotton, and handmade carpets.

Caspian oil

Oil rigs surround the shores of the Caspian Sea. Almost a century ago, these oilfields supplied half the world's petroleum. But the industry declined, and the water and soil became heavily polluted. New discoveries have brought another Caspian oil boom, as U.S., Russian, and Iranian companies compete for a share and plan new international pipelines. But oil wealth has yet to benefit the ordinary people of Central Asia. Many remain very poor in this land.

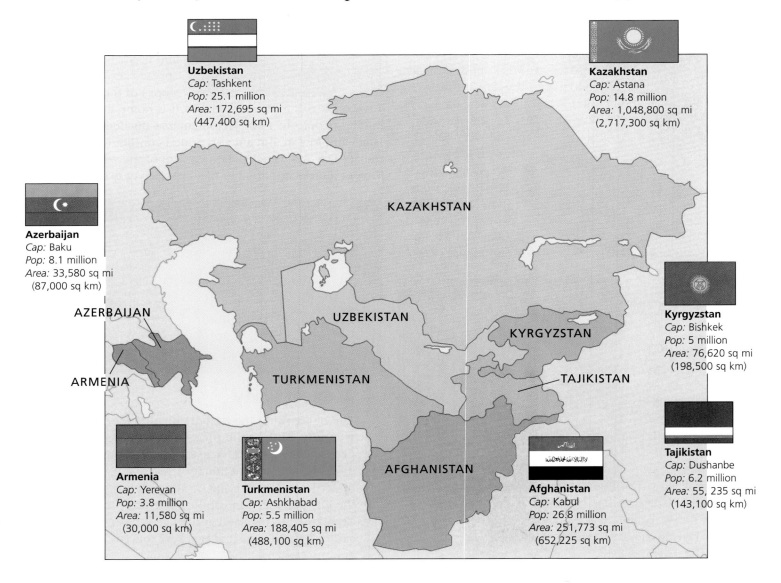

Uzbekistan
Cap: Tashkent
Pop: 25.1 million
Area: 172,695 sq mi
(447,400 sq km)

Kazakhstan
Cap: Astana
Pop: 14.8 million
Area: 1,048,800 sq mi
(2,717,300 sq km)

Azerbaijan
Cap: Baku
Pop: 8.1 million
Area: 33,580 sq mi
(87,000 sq km)

Kyrgyzstan
Cap: Bishkek
Pop: 5 million
Area: 76,620 sq mi
(198,500 sq km)

Armenia
Cap: Yerevan
Pop: 3.8 million
Area: 11,580 sq mi
(30,000 sq km)

Turkmenistan
Cap: Ashkhabad
Pop: 5.5 million
Area: 188,405 sq mi
(488,100 sq km)

Afghanistan
Cap: Kabul
Pop: 26.8 million
Area: 251,773 sq mi
(652,225 sq km)

Tajikistan
Cap: Dushanbe
Pop: 6.2 million
Area: 55, 235 sq mi
(143,100 sq km)

Peoples of Central Asia

Uzbek

Afghani

Churches and mosques

During Central Asia's Soviet period, religions were discouraged. Recent years have seen a religious revival throughout the newly independent countries. Armenia has one of the oldest Christian traditions, with its faithful following mainly the Eastern Orthodox form of the faith. Other peoples of the region are Muslims, attending the many fine mosques across the region.

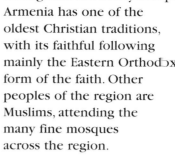

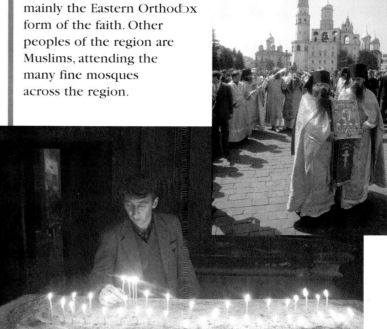

Many Central Asian peoples live nomadic lives, following their herds of sheep, goats, and camels from one pasture to another, often through very difficult and rugged terrain. Others lead more settled lives in villages and towns, benefiting from the development of heavy industry and the building of roads during the Soviet period (1950s-90s). The Armenians are a Caucasian people. The Azeris, Uzbeks, Turkmen, Kyrgyz, and the Uyghurs (of the Chinese borderlands) are all Turkic groups, speaking languages related to Turkish. Mongol groups include the Hazzara of eastern Afghanistan. The Tajiks and the Pashtun occupy large regions in the center and south of Afghanistan. These two groups are mostly of mixed origins and have descended from Caucasians, Mongols, and Aryans (peoples related to the Iranians).

Cotton fields

Although fertile farming land is scarce in Central Asia, its warm climate and irrigation projects make it possible to grow cotton on a large scale throughout the region. Uzbekistan is the fifth-largest cotton producer in the world, and many forms of cotton textiles are manufactured in its major cities.

Afghanistan

Afghanistan is a land of gorges, fast-flowing rivers, desert plains, and high mountain passes. Buses and trucks, often painted with ornate decoration, drive along the rough, zig-zagging roads that cling to the hillsides. Afghanistan lies on the route between Central Asia and India. It has been fought over and occupied for thousands of years, and conflict between rival warlords has added to the suffering of the population. The country was invaded by the Soviet Union in 1979, and was the scene of action by a U.S.-led coalition in 2001.

The yurt

The nomadic peoples of the Central Asian steppes live in quickly erected, dome-shaped tents known as yurts. The Kyrgyz, Kazakhs, Uzbeks, and Turkmen use one type in Mongolia and another in Siberia. A frame of willow poles supports a covering of dense felted material. Yurts offer warmth and comfort in extreme weather conditions.

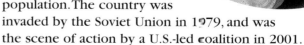

THE MIDDLE EAST

ASIA

The Middle East, in Southwest Asia, includes Saudi Arabia, Iraq, Iran, and six coastal states. They face the Persian Gulf or Indian Ocean.

Deserts stretch across the Arabian peninsula, which is bordered by the Red Sea, the Gulf, and the Indian Ocean. To the northwest, the Tigris and Euphrates Rivers bring water to parts of dry Iraq. In these fertile valleys, early humans learned to farm and began some of the world's earliest cities and nations. Iran (once known as Persia) was also the site of many ancient civilizations. It has large deserts, snowy mountain ranges, and farmland and pastures along its northern steppes. The politics of the region are dominated by its chief resource, oil, and by religion. Islam's holiest city, Mecca, is in Saudi Arabia. Mosques within the region represent the two main Muslim traditions of worship, known as Sunni and Shiah.

Cities and tents

Modern cities with high-rise buildings can be seen in some parts of the Middle East. However, the desert often begins just beyond the city limits. In such dry lands the old ways of life continue, with camel herders pitching tents in the traditional manner. Even so, the pace of change has been so rapid that many city dwellers still feel more at home in a tent. Many people often wear the traditional robes and headdresses of the desert nomads, which give cool comfort in the baking heat.

Ocean traders

The Yemeni and Omani Arabs have a long history of seafaring. Over the ages they used the seasonal monsoon winds to sail the Indian Ocean, trading in silks and spices from India and farther east, and in ivory, gold, and slaves from Africa. In 1699, they took over the island of Zanzibar and founded an East African coastal empire. Their wooden ships, known as dhows, were built in various sizes. All had the "lateen" triangular sail.

Iraq
Cap: Baghdad
Pop: 23.6 million
Area: 169,240 sq mi
(438,445 sq km)

Kuwait
Cap: Kuwait City
Pop: 2.3 million
Area: 9,370 sq mi
(24,280 sq km)

Bahrain
Cap: Manama
Pop: 700,000
Area: 255 sq mi
(661 sq km)

Qatar
Cap: Doha
Pop: 600,000
Area: 4,415 sq mi
(11,435 sq km)

Saudi Arabia
Cap: Riyadh
Pop: 21.1 million
Area: 849,425 sq mi
(2,200,000 sq km)

Yemen
Cap: Sana'a
Pop: 18 million
Area: 203,849 sq mi
(527,970 sq km)

Oman
Cap: Muscat
Pop: 2.4 million
Area: 104,970 sq mi
(271,950 sq km)

United Arab Emirates
Cap: Abu Dhabi
Pop: 3.3 million
Area: 29,010 sq mi
(75,150 sq km)

Iran
Cap: Tehran
Pop: 66.1 million
Area: 636,292 sq mi
(1,648,000 sq km)

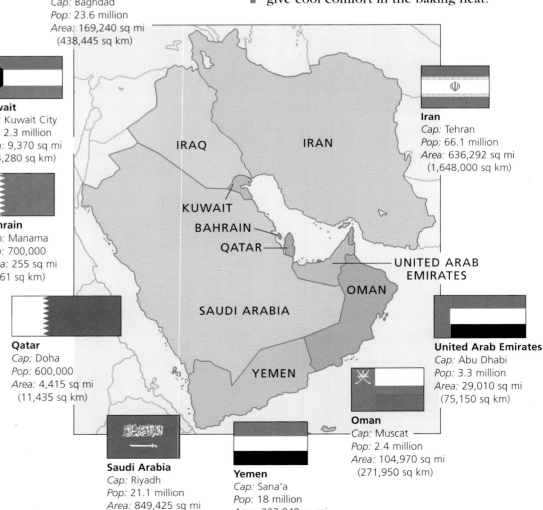

Peoples of the Middle East

Saudi Arabian

Iraqi

The peoples of Iraq, Saudi Arabia, Yemen, Oman, and the small Gulf states are predominantly of Arab origin. However, they have varying ways of life and traditions, from the nomadic Bedouin of the Arabian desert, to the Ma'adan or Marsh Arabs of southern Iraq. Aryan peoples include Iranians and the Kurds, who live in Iran, Iraq, and Turkey. The Kurds have long been campaigning for an independent homeland. The Iranians, known in ancient times as the Persians, speak dialects of the Farsi (Persian) language. Several related minorities also live in Iran, such as the Baluchis of the southeast and the Bakhtiari of the Zagros Mountains. There are also Turkic minorities, including a large number of Azeris. The oil wealth of the region has meant an influx of people from many other countries, including Europe and the Americas.

Home in the marshes

The Tigris and Euphrates rivers join in southern Iraq amid a broad area of marshy wetlands. The people who live here, the Ma'adan or Marsh Arabs, build artificial islands and floating houses of reeds, and travel by canoe or motorboat. They live by fishing, mat-making, and breeding water buffalo. As in many remote rural communities, the future of the Ma'adan is under threat. Their wetland areas are being drained for irrigation, their young people leave for the cities, and there has been conflict with Iraq's leaders in Baghdad.

"New lamps for old"

At the center of many older towns in the Middle East is the bazaar, a covered market or maze of narrow alleys. Traditional crafts on sale are reminders of well-known tales from the Middle Ages, such as *Aladdin* from *A Thousand and One Nights*. In the bazaar, gleaming copper lamps and coffee pots, silver jewelry, curved knives in sheaths, and embroidered textiles can be found. While a deal is agreed, customers may be served sweet, black coffee. The markets are also places to exchange news as people come in from the deserts—often in four-wheel drive cars, rather than camels.

Wealth from oil

Oil (petroleum) is sometimes called "black gold." As one of the most useful fuels and mineral resources in an energy-hungry world, oil brings great wealth to the desert nations around the Gulf—lands which have few other natural resources. Saudi Arabia is the world's biggest oil producer, and Iran, Iraq, the United Arab Emirates, and Kuwait are all in the top 15. Gigantic oil supertankers fill up from pipelines at coastal terminals and carry their cargo down the Gulf into the Indian Ocean, bound for the industrialized world.

Magic carpets

Carpets have been made in the Middle East and Central Asia for many centuries, and the Iranians and Kurds are expert at their craft. The carpets may be made from wool or silk knotted on strong threads of hemp or flax. They are hardwearing and beautiful, with various regional styles, colors, and patterns. Some are extremely valuable. Carpets first developed from the portable, roll-up floor coverings needed for nomadic life.

MOUNTAINS & PLAINS

ASIA

The Pamir and Himalayan mountain chains contain many of the world's highest summits. Their melting snows feed powerful rivers, which flow across the wide, dusty plains to the south.

The north of Pakistan reaches high into these mountain ranges. It is here that the Indus River turns southwest on its journey to the Arabian Sea, bringing water to the southern plains. More than half of all Pakistanis are farmers, but there are also large industrial cities, such as Lahore and the seaport of Karachi. From 1947, Bangladesh was part of the Pakistani state and known as East Pakistan, but it broke away in 1971 to become a separate nation. Its densely crowded agricultural land surrounds the great rivers of the Brahmaputra and Ganges, which form a delta to the south on the Bay of Bengal. Nepal and little Bhutan are two kingdoms set high in the mountains of the Himalayas.

Tilling the soil

The Indus and its tributaries form five main waterways in Pakistan's region of Punjab, supplying the world's biggest irrigation system. The Indus valley was farmed in prehistoric times, and great cities developed as early as 2500 B.C. Modern Pakistan grows wheat as its chief crop and also rice, sugarcane, corn, dates, and fruit. The food crops in Bangladesh are similar, but the farmland of the Ganges delta often suffers from floods which destroy villages and crops. Bhutan and Nepal grow rice in the south and hardy crops like potatoes on the valley floors and terraced hillsides of the Himalayas.

Cotton and jute

Pakistan is the fourth-largest producer of cotton in the world. Raw cotton is a major export, and the fibers are also supplied to the textile mills of Karachi and Lahore. After weaving and dyeing, finished cotton cloth and garments are exported around the world. Bangladesh is the world's biggest exporter of jute and jute products. This plant's coarse stems are soaked and beaten to provide long strands of tough, hard-wearing fiber. Jute is used to make materials such as sacking, burlap, and matting. The development of artificial fibers has reduced the need for both cotton and jute, forcing the growth of new industries.

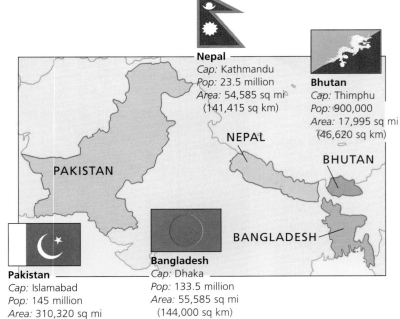

Nepal
Cap: Kathmandu
Pop: 23.5 million
Area: 54,585 sq mi
(141,415 sq km)

Bhutan
Cap: Thimphu
Pop: 900,000
Area: 17,995 sq mi
(46,620 sq km)

NEPAL

BHUTAN

PAKISTAN

BANGLADESH

Pakistan
Cap: Islamabad
Pop: 145 million
Area: 310,320 sq mi
(803,940 sq km)

Bangladesh
Cap: Dhaka
Pop: 133.5 million
Area: 55,585 sq mi
(144,000 sq km)

Peoples of the mountains and plains

Nepalese

Bhutanese

Most Pakistanis are Aryan peoples, related to their neighbors in Afghanistan to the west and northern India in the east. The largest group is that of Punjabis, but there are also large minorities of Sindhis, Baluchis, and Pashtun. Almost all of the people in Bangladesh—some 98 percent—are Bengalis. All these groups also have large communities living overseas, especially in Britain, which before 1947 ruled these two countries as part of India. Tibeto-Burman peoples live in the two Himalayan kingdoms. They include the Bhotias, Sherpas, Gurung, and Newars of Nepal and the Drukpas and Monpas of Bhutan. There are Tibetan minorities in both Himalayan countries, and a large Nepalese community in Bhutan. Strong links between India and Nepal mean that there is a constant interchange of traders and travelers.

Three faiths

Buddhist temples may be seen in many villages and towns of Nepal and Bhutan. Above them are fluttering flags, each representing a prayer. Holy texts are also written on cylinders, which are spun around by the pilgrims. Young boys who become monks shave their heads and dress in monastic robes. They learn the ancient Buddhist way of life. Nepal also has many sacred Hindu sites and temples. Islam is the faith with the most followers in the region. About 97 percent of Pakistanis and 83 percent of Bangladeshis are Muslims.

Living in the Himalayas

The Sherpas are a mountain people—relatively short of stature, wiry, and very tough. They are among the world's best trekkers, hikers, and climbers, able to carry heavy loads over rough terrain. A Sherpa named Tenzing Norgay was one of the first two people to scale Mount Everest, the world's highest peak, in 1953. Many Sherpas act as guides to the foreign rock-climbers, hillwalkers, and mountaineers who now visit Nepal. Himalayan villages are built of clay bricks or stone. Villagers may eat rice and lentils and drink tea flavored with butter and salt. Even the highest mountain passes of the region are grazed by long-haired types of incredibly hardy cattle called yaks. Traditionally these provided many of life's needs, including wool, milk, meat, hides, and horns and bones for carving and utensils.

Skilled fingers

In Nepal and Bhutan, many ordinary windows, shutters, and doors, as well as grand temples and palace buildings, display beautiful wood carvings. Other mountain crafts include traditional ornamental work in silver and bronze, stone, and reed. The disputed region of Kashmir, which is currently divided by the borders of Pakistan, India, and China, is famous for its warm shawls, finely woven from the soft "cashmere" wool taken from a special breed of goat. Over 4,000 years ago, magnificent jewelry, carved heads, and clay models were already being produced in the Indus valley. Lowland regions of modern Pakistan, such as Sind, produce embroidery, patchwork textiles, and quilts in bold colors. Bangladeshi craft work also includes a type of decorative, stitched quilt called a *kantha*. These quilts may be patterned with intricate designs of leaves, flowers, animals, or people.

INDIA AND THE SOUTH

India forms a great triangle to the south of the Himalayas. The island nations of Sri Lanka and the Maldives lie in the Indian Ocean.

India has snow-covered mountains, broad dusty plains, burning deserts, and lush tropical vegetation. The climate is often very hot and dry, relieved only by seasonal monsoon winds which bring tropical storms and torrents of rain from the ocean. India has the second-largest population in the world— a fascinating mixture of ethnic groups, languages, religions, and customs. Many people are poor country farmers and laborers. Some pour into great cities such as Calcutta or Mumbai (Bombay) to seek work and food. The world's biggest producer of tea, India also grows rice, sugarcane, cotton, and jute. Major industries include the manufacture of chemicals, textiles, and vehicles.

Sri Lanka is an island of green forests, hills, and coconut groves. It has coastal fisheries and exports tea, rubber, and textiles. The Maldives, a long chain of coral islands in the Indian Ocean, are so low-lying that they are at risk of being submerged should sea levels rise.

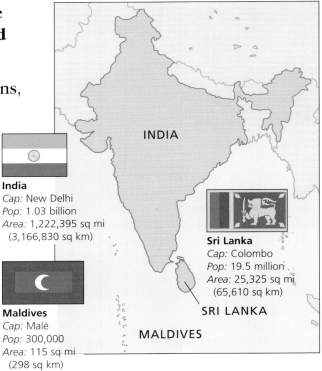

India
Cap: New Delhi
Pop: 1.03 billion
Area: 1,222,395 sq mi
(3,166,830 sq km)

Maldives
Cap: Malé
Pop: 300,000
Area: 115 sq mi
(298 sq km)

Sri Lanka
Cap: Colombo
Pop: 19.5 million
Area: 25,325 sq mi
(65,610 sq km)

Brilliant colors

Colorful dyes are sold in markets all over India. Garments and costumes can dazzle the eye, with many men wearing plain, bright white cotton clothes, while many women dress in blues, reds, pinks, greens, and yellows. The Indian dress, called a sari, is a long length of cotton or silk wrapped around the body and tucked into itself. In the northwest state of Rajasthan, dresses are embroidered with mirror sequins.

Taj Mahal

In 1631, the Moghuls—Muslims of Mongol descent—ruled much of India. During the reign of Emperor Shah Jahan, his wife died. Her royal title was Mumtaz Mahal. The grieving emperor had a monument built in memory of his beloved wife, at the city of Agra, by the Yamuna River in central northern India. The building was called the Taj Mahal. Made of smooth white marble and decorated with precious stones, it was completed in 1653. The Taj Mahal still stands today, gleaming and serene. Many declare it to be the most beautiful building they have ever seen.

Peoples of India and the south

Indian

Sinhalese

The many peoples of India are of mixed origin. About 845 different languages and dialects are spoken in the great country, including English. Some groups, such as the Bhils, are descendants of India's first inhabitants. The Naga and some other groups are related to Tibetans and Burmans. Many southern Indians are of Dravidian origin, such as the speakers of Tamil, Kannadu, and Malayalam. Paler-skinned northerners are usually of Aryan descent—later arrivals who speak languages related to those of Iran and Europe. Both northern and southern groups have mingled and intermarried over the ages. Followers of the Hindu faith are often identified by the social status of their family, called their caste. Muslims, Sikhs, Jains, or Parsees are also mainly identified by religious background. Sri Lanka is home to the Tamils and the Sinhalese, who also settled the Maldives.

Rice and spice

Rice and lentils are sold in the market and form the basis of many Indian meals. Indian breads include white leavened bread called nan (naan), unleavened wheat pancakes known as chapatis, and fried breads such as puris and parathas. Meat, fish, and chicken are eaten, but many dishes are vegetarian. Most are curries, made with spices such as pepper, chili, ginger, cumin, coriander, saffron, and cardamom. Tropical fruits such as bananas and mangoes are widely available. Indian sweets, some made with carrot and milk, are sticky and brightly colored.

Travel by train

Long-distance and suburban travel in India is often by train. Some railroad carriages are modern and air-conditioned, but most are old-fashioned, pulled by steam locomotives. Cheaper carriages are very crowded, and sometimes passengers cling to the sides and roofs of the trains. Much of the Indian rail network dates back to the days when India was part of the British Empire (1858–1947).

The holy river

At the riverside town of Varanasi, or Benares, Hindu pilgrims bathe in the waters of the Ganges River. To people of the Hindu faith, this river is sacred. It rises in the mountains of the Himalayas, where it is fed by melting snows. By the time it has reached the plains of northern India, it is wide, slow, and winding. When they die, many Hindus choose to be cremated beside the Ganges and to have their ashes cast into the waters of this holy river.

Many faiths

In India, cows are sacred and are left to wander city streets. A land of many religions, India is filled with temples and mosques. For Hindus, the characteristics of God are expressed in their different gods and goddesses. Hindus believe that all living creatures go through reincarnation, or rebirth, after they die. Buddhists believe in reincarnation and in the holiness of life. Jains go to extreme lengths to protect living things. India has the world's second-largest Muslim population. The Sikh religion began in the 1500s as an attempt to build bridges between Islam and Hinduism. Male Sikhs bind their long hair in a cloth called a turban.

SOUTHEAST ASIA

The Asian mainland reaches southward between the Indian and the Pacific Oceans, ending in a long peninsula and a trail of island chains.

Southeast Asia is a tropical region with broad river valleys, forests, and paddy fields planted with rice. Its large cities, such as Singapore and Kuala Lumpur, are centers of international business. Southeast Asia has many tourist resorts and beautiful beaches, countless small farming villages, ancient temples, and shrines. Rich in culture, the region is known for its graceful dances, wood carving, and dyed textiles.

Between the 1500s and 1800s, much of Southeast Asia was colonized by European powers eager to profit from the spice trade and rubber plantations. Over the past 50 years, some countries of the region have struggled to gain independence, amidst terrible wars and political unrest. Resources today include oil, nickel, tin, and tropical hardwood timber from the shrinking forests.

Angkor Wat

From the 1100s to the 1400s, Cambodia was ruled by the great Khmer Empire. The huge city of Angkor Thom was the capital of this mighty power, which honored both Hindu and Buddhist religious traditions. The city had many temples and shrines, the biggest being Angkor Wat. Abandoned and overgrown by the jungle, the vast temple was rediscovered in 1861.

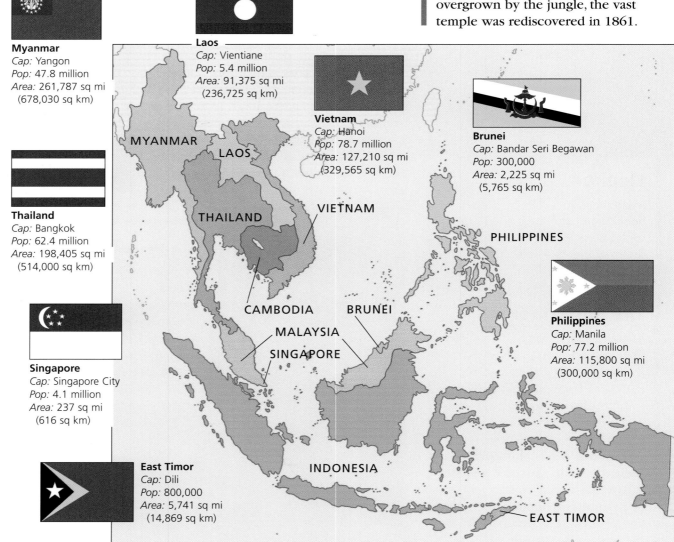

Myanmar
Cap: Yangon
Pop: 47.8 million
Area: 261,787 sq mi
(678,030 sq km)

Laos
Cap: Vientiane
Pop: 5.4 million
Area: 91,375 sq mi
(236,725 sq km)

Vietnam
Cap: Hanoi
Pop: 78.7 million
Area: 127,210 sq mi
(329,565 sq km)

Brunei
Cap: Bandar Seri Begawan
Pop: 300,000
Area: 2,225 sq mi
(5,765 sq km)

Cambodia
Cap: Phnom Penh
Pop: 13.1 million
Area: 69,865 sq mi
(181,000 sq km)

Thailand
Cap: Bangkok
Pop: 62.4 million
Area: 198,405 sq mi
(514,000 sq km)

Malaysia
Cap: Kuala Lumpur
Pop: 22.7 million
Area: 128,525 sq mi
(332,965 sq km)

Singapore
Cap: Singapore City
Pop: 4.1 million
Area: 237 sq mi
(616 sq km)

Philippines
Cap: Manila
Pop: 77.2 million
Area: 115,800 sq mi
(300,000 sq km)

Indonesia
Cap: Jakarta
Pop: 206.1 million
Area: 779,000 sq mi
(1,919,569 sq km)

East Timor
Cap: Dili
Pop: 800,000
Area: 5,741 sq mi
(14,869 sq km)

Peoples of Southeast Asia

Thai

Indonesian

For thousands of years, various groups of people from the great civilizations of China have sailed or migrated south and settled in many parts of Southeast Asia. They make up 76 percent of the population in Singapore, which also has large Indian communities. Tibeto-Burman peoples include the Burmese, Kachin, and Karen of Myanmar (formerly named Burma). Thai peoples include the Shan of Myanmar, the Thai and Yuan of Thailand, and the Lao of Laos. The Hmong people living south of the Chinese frontier are members of the Miao-Yao language family. Austro-Asiatic language speakers include the Khmer of Cambodia, the Vietnamese, Malaysians, Indonesians, and the Filipinos of the Philippines. Within these groups there are many different cultures and ethnic groups, including the Dayaks and Iban of Borneo.

Cane craft

Southeast Asian crafts and export items are often made from cane, like the shades at this workshop in Thailand. Craft workers use canes made of bamboo, a woody-stemmed grass, or rattan. Strong yet flexible, rattan is cut from the thorny stem of a climbing plant called the rattan palm, which grows in dense thickets in rain forests. From Java to the Philippines, it is used to make trays, screens, chairs, tables, stools, baskets, and other items, for home use and sale.

Elephant power

Asian elephants of India and Southeast Asia have been tamed and taught to carry out a number of useful tasks. Their power can shift huge logs, and their wide feet do little damage compared to huge vehicles. Asian elephants were moving heavy tree trunks in Myanmar long before modern hydraulic machinery was invented.

Floating markets

Fresh vegetables and tropical fruits may be bought at markets almost everywhere, in villages, towns, and modern cities. Much produce is sold directly from boats moored along the banks of rivers and canals. Rice or noodles form the basis of most Southeast Asian meals, and cassava (also known as tapioca) is also eaten. Chicken dishes are popular, as are seafoods like shrimps and fish. Some meals are flavored with chili, lemongrass, coconut, or satay (peanut sauce).

Manila

The Philippine capital of Manila, located on Luzon Island's Manila Bay, bustles with more than 1.6 million people. Industries include sugar refining, textiles, and coconut processing. Spanish colonizers founded Manila in 1571, but most people here are Filipinos. One Spanish legacy is religion. Over 80 percent of the Philippines is Roman Catholic.

Archipelago

Indonesia contains 13,600 islands including Irian Jaya, Sumatra, Java, and Kalimantan. Islam and Hinduism are the major religions but they are influenced by the local belief in ancestral and natural spirits. The Balinese dance *legong* is performed by 2 or 3 girls and tells an ancient story of love and battle.

CHINA, TAIWAN, MONGOLIA

China is a huge country, about the size of Western Europe. In the far north, the winters are bitterly cold and snowy, while the south is warm and humid with tropical rainstorms. The west is a dry region of mountains and deserts.

China has the largest population in the world. Most people live in the eastern half of the country, where the great rivers of the Huang and Chang wind across fertile, intensively farmed plains to the Yellow Sea and East China Sea. Great cities, ports, and factories bustle with millions of people. The west is more empty and remote, and includes the vast, bleak plateau of Tibet.

Mongolia is an independent nation, although part of the Mongol homelands lies within Chinese borders. Mongolia contrasts greatly with China, being sparsely populated, with endless windy steppes and deserts which can be baking hot or freezing cold.

Land of history

The Great Wall was built to defend China's northern borders. China was ruled by emperors for over 2,000 years. It produced wonderful paintings, pottery, and poetry, as well as many important inventions. The empire ended in 1911. In 1948, Mao Zedong led the Chinese Communist Party (CCP) to power. Mao's portrait still fronts the old imperial palace. The CCP still governs, but many communist policies have been abandoned.

Hong Kong

Many of China's modern cities dazzle with bright lights—none more so than Hong Kong. This former British island colony and international business center was returned to Chinese rule in 1997. It lies off the southern coast of China, near Guangzhou (Canton).

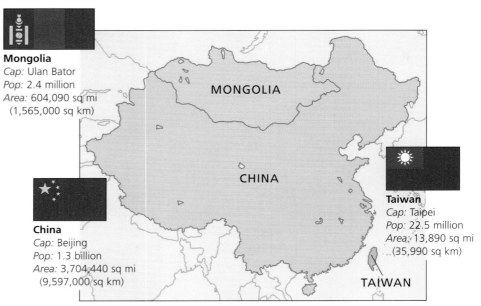

Mongolia
Cap: Ulan Bator
Pop: 2.4 million
Area: 604,090 sq mi
(1,565,000 sq km)

China
Cap: Beijing
Pop: 1.3 billion
Area: 3,704,440 sq mi
(9,597,000 sq km)

Taiwan
Cap: Taipei
Pop: 22.5 million
Area: 13,890 sq mi
(35,990 sq km)

MONGOLIA

CHINA

TAIWAN

Peoples of China, Taiwan, Mongolia

Mongol

Tibetan

Most people in China and Taiwan belong to the Han Chinese ethnic group, which also includes the Muslim Hui. More people speak the Standard Chinese language than any other language in the world. Many Han speak very different dialects, such as Cantonese. The remaining 7 percent of the Chinese people occupy over half the country by area, and belong to many different ethnic groups. Tai peoples include the Zhuang, Li, and Dong. Tibeto-Burmans include the Yi and the Tibetans, many of whom wish independence for their homeland. The Miao-Yao peoples form another ethnic group, which numbers several million. Many Turkic peoples live in the northwest and Manchus in the northeast. Mongols of the Chakhar, Korchin, Dagur, and Torgut groups live in China, while the Khalkha Mongols live in Mongolia.

Farm foods

The eastern half of China has so many people that every river, lake, and coast is fished, and every tiny patch of land is sown with food crops. In the cool north these include wheat, fruit, and root vegetables. Southern crops are rice, corn, sugarcane, and tropical fruits. The dry northwest depends heavily on irrigation. Tibetans produce barley and herd shaggy wild cattle called yaks. Mongolians, too, are primarily herders. They keep sheep, goats, and Bactrian (two-humped) camels on the grassy steppes.

Taiwan

Taiwan is a crowded, prosperous island off the southeast coast of the Chinese mainland. Most of its people are Chinese. In the 1920s–40s, there was bitter fighting across China, between Communists, Nationalists, and Japanese invaders. When the Communists won the war in 1948, Nationalist leaders fled to Taiwan and set up an alternative government. Today, China claims Taiwan as part of its territory, but the Taiwanese government maintains some independence.

The Silk Road

An ancient trading route known as the Silk Road runs westward from northern China. It passes through the lands of Central Asia to the Near East, and on to Europe. Along its remote tracks, camels and ponies carried Chinese exports to the west, including bales of silk, spices, and hard "bricks" of tea leaves. Gradually more goods were transported west by sailing ships, rather than by road. But the old route can still be traveled today, by overland vehicle.

Street chefs

Chinese cooking takes place on the street and in markets and yards, as well as in restaurants. Some dishes are steamed slowly, others are stir-fried at great heat. Noodles are common in the north, and rice in the south. Each region has its own special dishes. Ingredients include pork, duck, fish, shellfish, chilies, garlic, greens, and scallions. Chinese cooking has become popular all over the world.

Three faiths

Buddhist monasteries can be seen across Mongolia and Tibet. In much of China, Buddhism has merged with two other ancient faiths—the teachings of Confucius, which orders social harmony, and Taoism, which follows the flow of nature. Over the ages these faiths intertwined with old beliefs in spirits. The CCP discouraged worship, but temples are now being restored.

69

JAPAN & KOREA

The Sea of Japan is an inlet of the Pacific Ocean, bordering the Korean peninsula and the islands of Japan. These include Hokkaido, Honshu, Shikoku, and Kyushu.

Although the Koreans are a single people, since the end of the Korean War in 1953, their homeland has been divided into two rival states. North Korea is run by the communist Korean Workers' Party (KWP). South Korea has strong economic links with the U.S. and Europe, with a democratic government since 1987.

Japan is also a democracy, with the emperor as head of state. Its islands are mountainous and prone to earthquakes; most people live on coastal lowlands. The merging cities of Tokyo, Yokohama, and Kawasaki have a population of 35 million.

Fishing and rice are important across the region. Many people in North Korea are poor, but South Korea and Japan have become industrial giants, producing vehicles and a vast array of electronic goods. However, like other developed Asian nations, they have faced recent economic problems.

Simple and elegant

Japan has a long tradition of arts and crafts. Throughout its history, styles of painting and woodblock printing have remained simple yet elegant, even when showing busy scenes of daily life. The same simplicity is clear in pottery and porcelain, and also in traditional architecture, which is deceptively plain and uncluttered. The trend even extends to the country's poetry, with deep emotions expressed within one brief phrase. Japan has inspired artists, craft workers, designers, architects, and writers in many other parts of the world.

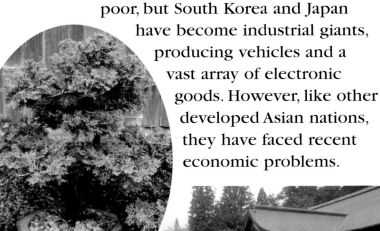

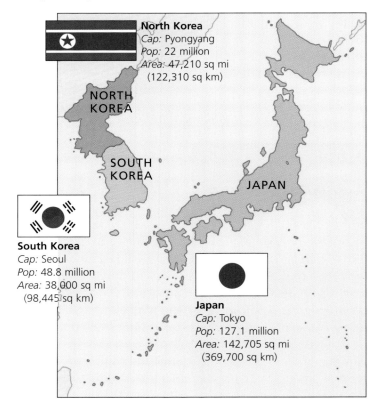

North Korea
Cap: Pyongyang
Pop: 22 million
Area: 47,210 sq mi
(122,310 sq km)

South Korea
Cap: Seoul
Pop: 48.8 million
Area: 38,000 sq mi
(98,445 sq km)

Japan
Cap: Tokyo
Pop: 127.1 million
Area: 142,705 sq mi
(369,700 sq km)

Spiritual gardens

Japanese gardens have been influenced by both Shinto (a religion which respects the forces of nature) and Zen (a strict sect of Buddhism). Gardens are simply designed, quite often with raked sand or gravel, ponds, and pools with fish, and trees miniaturized by pruning and potting in the bonsai style. Many religious shrines are set among flowering trees for peace and serenity. In Japan, flower arrangement is prized as a serious form of art.

Peoples of the Far East

Korean

Japanese

The histories of both Korea and Japan extend back thousands of years. Over the ages, both countries have seen their cultures influenced by their Chinese neighbors. The Japanese and Korean languages may be distantly related, and there is also a possible link with the Altaic language family of Central Asia and Siberia. The Korean language has about 78 million speakers worldwide. Koreans live throughout Korea and in many other lands, including Japan and China. In Japan, 99 percent of the population is ethnically Japanese. There are also strong Japanese communities in many other parts of the world, and Japanese speakers number about 135 million worldwide. Among Japan's earliest inhabitants, the Ainu people survive mainly in the north of the northernmost island, Hokkaido. However, they number only about 15,000.

Speedy rails

In Taejon, South Korea, monorail cars transport passengers rapidly, high above the crowded streets. The ultra-fast bullet trains, known as *Shinkansen*, are a popular method of transportation in Japan. Trains offer the most efficient form of travel through the undulating Japanese landscape. The country will soon have five of the world's ten longest rail tunnels. The Seikan tunnel links the islands of Hokkaido and Honshu and is 33.5 mi (53.9 km) long.

Ancient and modern

With its bright lights and busy city streets, Japan is one of the world's most modern, high-tech nations. It is also a land of history and tradition. Many women still wear the traditional silk robe, or kimono. Festivals reenact the days when samurai (Japan's medieval knights) galloped across the country, laid castles to siege, and battled with valor and loyalty. The samurai used to train for war by fighting with sticks instead of their deadly swords. This was the origin of kendo, one of Japan's many martial arts. Judo and sumo (heavyweight wrestling) are also popular.

Kimchi and rice

Korean produce is sold direct from grower to consumer, in markets in almost every village and city. The Korean peninsula has warm summers but bitterly cold winters, and only one-sixth of the land is suitable for raising crops. These include soybeans, green vegetables, corn, barley, potatoes, and sweet potatoes. Rice is the basis of most meals in both North and South Korea. Dried fish, chicken, duck, beef, and pork are popular, as are soups, noodles, and kimchi— a strong type of pickle.

City life

Business has long been a way of life in Japan. Its companies pay their workers well, look after their needs, and expect great loyalty in return. Japan quickly rebuilt its economy after defeat in World War II. Japan was a pioneer in developing the electronic micro-technology now in global use. After a hard day's work, many office staff like to relax in an arcade by playing *pachinko*, a form of pinball, or by singing karaoke-style.

71

AFRICA

Africa is the second-largest continent in the world. It lies between the Mediterranean Sea, the Red Sea, the Atlantic Ocean, and the Indian Ocean. The northern shores enjoy a warm climate, and where there is enough moisture, citrus fruits can be grown. However, huge bands of desert straddle the continent, from the great Sahara in the north to the Namib and Kalahari in the south. In many regions there are areas of grassland with scattered trees, known as savannah. Rain forests cover parts of West Africa and the basin of the Congo River. The Great Rift Valley runs down the east of the continent, its course marked by a chain of large lakes.

In ancient times, Africa had many kingdoms and empires. Its deserts, mountains, fierce heat, and wild animals made travel difficult, and some regions were unknown to the rest of the world until the 1800s. Then much of Africa was seized by European powers, who cared little for the needs of local people. Many Africans were sold as slaves by European and Arab traders. Today, most of the continent is made up of free, independent nations, with many peoples and cultures. Wars, floods, and famines have caused great suffering, but Africans work toward building a better future.

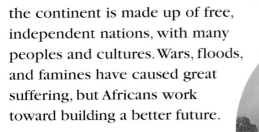

African trade

Busy public markets are found in almost every African town. All kinds of products are traded, from fruit and vegetables to live animals, canned fish, bicycle tires, watches, and detergents. Some African nations face great economic problems. They had little choice but to borrow money in order to develop their countries, and now face crippling repayments for these debts.

Ancient Egypt

The awesome monuments of ancient Egypt, such as the pyramids at Giza and the temple of Pharaoh Ramses II at Abu Simbel, are still impressing visitors today. Ancient Egypt was Africa's first great civilization and flourished from about 5,100 to 3,100 years ago. Its rulers, called pharaohs, conquered and traded with neighboring lands. The Egyptians produced wonderful jewelry, furniture, and paintings, many of which survived in royal tombs.

Building a new Africa

In many African villages, daily life has changed little in centuries. Food is grown, processed and cooked, and houses are built, all by the villagers themselves. Today, Africa's needs include better schools and education, sufficient healthy food, clean water, and improved healthcare. African nations meet as an alliance, the Organization of African Unity (OAU), to discuss political and economic policies.

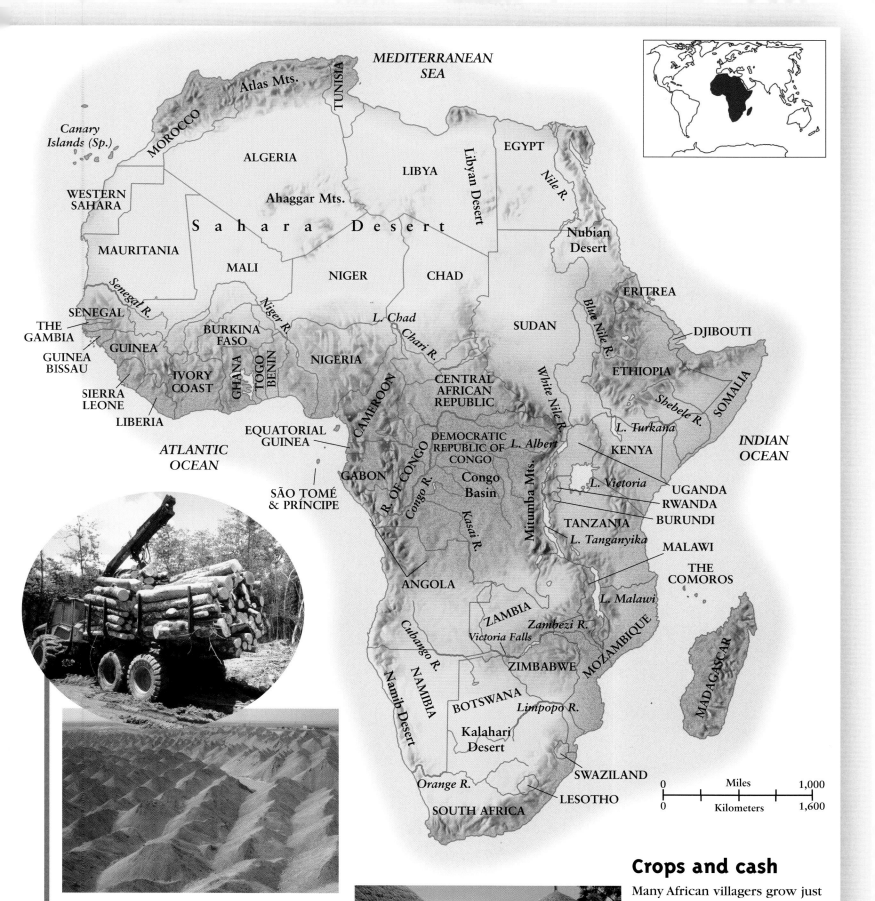

MEDITERRANEAN SEA

TUNISIA

Atlas Mts.

MOROCCO

Canary Islands (Sp.)

WESTERN SAHARA

ALGERIA

LIBYA

EGYPT

Libyan Desert

Nile R.

Ahaggar Mts.

S a h a r a   D e s e r t

Nubian Desert

MAURITANIA

MALI

NIGER

CHAD

SUDAN

ERITREA

Senegal R.

SENEGAL

THE GAMBIA

GUINEA BISSAU

GUINEA

BURKINA FASO

Niger R.

L. Chad

Chari R.

Blue Nile R.

DJIBOUTI

ETHIOPIA

SOMALIA

Shebele R.

IVORY COAST

GHANA

TOGO

BENIN

NIGERIA

CENTRAL AFRICAN REPUBLIC

White Nile R.

SIERRA LEONE

LIBERIA

ATLANTIC OCEAN

EQUATORIAL GUINEA

CAMEROON

GABON

R. OF CONGO

Congo R.

DEMOCRATIC REPUBLIC OF CONGO

Congo Basin

L. Albert

Mitumba Mts.

L. Turkana

KENYA

L. Victoria

UGANDA

RWANDA

BURUNDI

INDIAN OCEAN

SÃO TOMÉ & PRÍNCIPE

Kasai R.

TANZANIA

L. Tanganyika

MALAWI

THE COMOROS

ANGOLA

L. Malawi

ZAMBIA

Zambezi R.

Victoria Falls

Cubango R.

MOZAMBIQUE

MADAGASCAR

Namib Desert

NAMIBIA

ZIMBABWE

BOTSWANA

Limpopo R.

Kalahari Desert

Orange R.

SWAZILAND

LESOTHO

SOUTH AFRICA

| 0 | Miles | 1,000 |
| 0 | Kilometers | 1,600 |

Africa's resources

Some parts of Africa are rich in natural resources. Hardwood timber is cut in the rain forests of the Congo River basin, despite concerns that logging is destroying the natural environment. Although the Sahara Desert is barren, it does provide mineral salts called phosphates, which are used to make fertilizers. Sierra Leone is rich in diamonds, and South Africa has the world's greatest gold mines. Nigeria has important oilfields in the region around the delta of the Niger River.

Crops and cash

Many African villagers grow just enough corn, millet, plantains (cooking bananas), or yams for themselves. Others work on larger farms, often owned by international firms. Their crops are sold for money rather than used locally. Exports include peanuts, coffee, tea, tropical fruits, green vegetables, tobacco, and sisal—a fiber used to make matting and twine.

73

NORTH AFRICA

North Africa borders the Mediterranean and Red Seas, and the Atlantic Ocean. Its northwest is known as the Maghreb, its south as the Sahel.

The Mediterranean coastal lands produce citrus fruits, olives, grapes, and barley. Goats and sheep are herded in the Atlas Mountains. Egypt grows cotton, rice, and beans, and Morocco is famed for its leather.

The Sahara Desert endures extremely high temperatures and runs across most of North Africa. The Nile River, on its route from Central Africa to the Mediterranean, flows through swamps in southern Sudan and forms a narrow lifeline through deserts in northern Sudan and Egypt.

Oases are pockets of green land around desert water holes. Saharan oases produce dates, figs, and melons. But the land beyond is barren. Some minerals are mined, such as phosphates in Morocco and the Western Sahara. Also, the desert is slowly spreading southward into the lands of the Sahel. Droughts can last for years on end, killing off the thin pasture on which herds of cattle depend. Here are some of the poorest nations on Earth.

The Nile River

Wooden sailing boats called feluccas sail the Egyptian section of the Nile River. Without this important river, the world's longest, Egypt would not exist. For thousands of years its annual flood waters left behind thick black mud on the riverbanks. This became fertile soil for growing the crops that provided food for the ancient Egyptians. The green strip through the desert is very narrow, but fans out over a large area near the Mediterranean coast, where the river forms a delta.

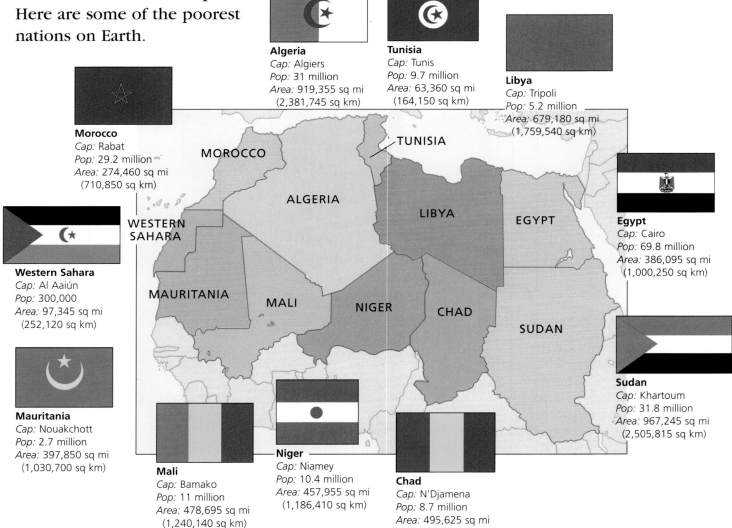

Algeria
Cap: Algiers
Pop: 31 million
Area: 919,355 sq mi
(2,381,745 sq km)

Tunisia
Cap: Tunis
Pop: 9.7 million
Area: 63,360 sq mi
(164,150 sq km)

Libya
Cap: Tripoli
Pop: 5.2 million
Area: 679,180 sq mi
(1,759,540 sq km)

Morocco
Cap: Rabat
Pop: 29.2 million
Area: 274,460 sq mi
(710,850 sq km)

Egypt
Cap: Cairo
Pop: 69.8 million
Area: 386,095 sq mi
(1,000,250 sq km)

Western Sahara
Cap: Al Aaiún
Pop: 300,000
Area: 97,345 sq mi
(252,120 sq km)

Sudan
Cap: Khartoum
Pop: 31.8 million
Area: 967,245 sq mi
(2,505,815 sq km)

Mauritania
Cap: Nouakchott
Pop: 2.7 million
Area: 397,850 sq mi
(1,030,700 sq km)

Mali
Cap: Bamako
Pop: 11 million
Area: 478,695 sq mi
(1,240,140 sq km)

Niger
Cap: Niamey
Pop: 10.4 million
Area: 457,955 sq mi
(1,186,410 sq km)

Chad
Cap: N'Djamena
Pop: 8.7 million
Area: 495,625 sq mi
(1,284,000 sq km)

Peoples of North Africa

Egyptian

Berber

The Berber peoples are probably the earliest surviving inhabitants of northwest Africa. Today, the greatest number of them live in Morocco and Algeria. They form many different groups, such as the Kabyle, the Zenatiya, the Tashelheyt, and the Tuareg. Arabs invaded the far north of Africa in the 600s and 700s, and now form the majority of the population throughout that region. The Arabs also mixed with local peoples in northern Sudan. Black Africa, where people generally have much darker skin, begins south of the Sahara. Peoples of the western Sahel include the Fulani, Hausa, Malinke, Dogon, Songhai, and Kanuri. In southern Sudan are the Shilluk, Nuer, and Dinka. A huge variety of languages may be heard throughout the region, belonging mainly to the Niger-Kordofanian and Nilo-Saharan families of language.

Arches and courtyards

Over the ages, the Muslim Arabs and Berbers of the north have built beautiful mosques and other religious buildings, as well as strongholds and forts, walled cities with mazes of tiny streets, and covered markets or souks. In lands where it rarely rains, such as Egypt, the roofs are flat. They may serve as an extra floor where people can sleep in the cool night air. South of the Sahara, the traditional architecture includes large mud buildings and villages of huts thatched with grass or reeds.

Henna patterns

Henna is a reddish-brown dye, which is made from the powdered leaves of a shrub called Egyptian privet. It is used as a hair dye and cosmetic. In North Africa and parts of East Africa it is used to paint intricate patterns on the hands and feet of women, especially for weddings and other celebrations. The swirling styles of the patterns are unique to each locality.

Living in the desert

The heat in the Sahara is fierce and the soil is barren and dry. The wind blows up storms of sand and grit. However, people do cross the desert and some even live around its fringes. The Bedouin are nomads of the Sahara and Arabian deserts. They lead their herds of goats, camels, and sheep from one oasis to another. The Tuareg trade between North and West Africa, wearing robes and veils against the heat and dust. Their dromedary (one-humped) camels are perfectly adapted to desert survival. Shelter is provided by quickly erected tents. Bedouin and some Berbers live in tents of woven goat hair, while those of the Tuareg are made from goat skin or palm matting.

Tagines and couscous

Cooking in northwest Africa makes use of many different flavorings and spices, such as ginger, coriander, almond, garlic, and saffron. Stews of lamb or vegetables are popular, and are known as *tagines* after the dishes in which they are cooked. Many meals are served with *couscous*, a kind of cracked, steamed wheat. In Egypt, beans in olive oil *(ful)* are a basic food. Mint tea and thick black coffee are drunk in cafés throughout North Africa. In the lands south of the Sahara, hot cereals and breads may be made of millet flour, and the many varieties of stews are usually very hot and spicy. However, in these areas of little rain and thin soil, failed crops and hunger are all too common.

WEST AFRICA

AFRICA

The West African coast curves north around the shores of the Gulf of Guinea, before bulging westward into the Atlantic Ocean.

West African coastal regions have a generally hot and humid climate. This was mainly a rain forest zone, but large areas have now been converted to tropical crops, producing peanuts, cacao beans (for making chocolate), and palm oil. There are many large seaports and industrial cities. The central west-east belt, away from the coast, is made up of savannah grasslands and rocky plateaus. The northern strip borders the arid lands of the Sahel region, and has seasonal cool winds. Goats and cattle are herded on its scant pasture.

West Africa suffered greatly from the 1500s, due to the exploits of European powers. Countless Africans were shipped to the Americas as slaves. The region was colonized more permanently by Europeans from the 1800s. But independence in the 1960s was followed by political strife and war. The region is rich in resources, including oil, diamonds, and gold.

Ancient beliefs

Most southern West Africans are Christians and most northerners are Muslims. However, traditional beliefs in the spirits of ancestors, and in the natural world, are still common throughout Africa, flourishing alongside the newer religions. At funerals and other important ceremonies in Burkina Faso, dancers wear masks and costumes representing spirits or animals.

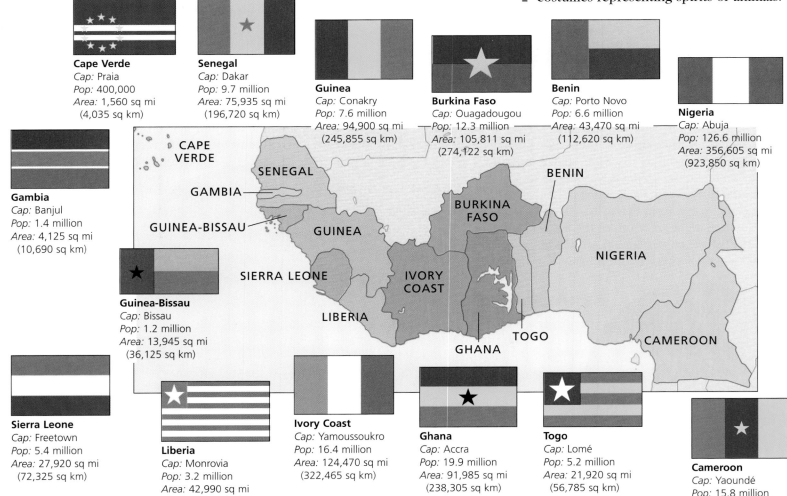

Cape Verde
Cap: Praia
Pop: 400,000
Area: 1,560 sq mi
(4,035 sq km)

Senegal
Cap: Dakar
Pop: 9.7 million
Area: 75,935 sq mi
(196,720 sq km)

Guinea
Cap: Conakry
Pop: 7.6 million
Area: 94,900 sq mi
(245,855 sq km)

Burkina Faso
Cap: Ouagadougou
Pop: 12.3 million
Area: 105,811 sq mi
(274,122 sq km)

Benin
Cap: Porto Novo
Pop: 6.6 million
Area: 43,470 sq mi
(112,620 sq km)

Nigeria
Cap: Abuja
Pop: 126.6 million
Area: 356,605 sq mi
(923,850 sq km)

Gambia
Cap: Banjul
Pop: 1.4 million
Area: 4,125 sq mi
(10,690 sq km)

Guinea-Bissau
Cap: Bissau
Pop: 1.2 million
Area: 13,945 sq mi
(36,125 sq km)

Sierra Leone
Cap: Freetown
Pop: 5.4 million
Area: 27,920 sq mi
(72,325 sq km)

Liberia
Cap: Monrovia
Pop: 3.2 million
Area: 42,990 sq mi
(111,370 sq km)

Ivory Coast
Cap: Yamoussoukro
Pop: 16.4 million
Area: 124,470 sq mi
(322,465 sq km)

Ghana
Cap: Accra
Pop: 19.9 million
Area: 91,985 sq mi
(238,305 sq km)

Togo
Cap: Lomé
Pop: 5.2 million
Area: 21,920 sq mi
(56,785 sq km)

Cameroon
Cap: Yaoundé
Pop: 15.8 million
Area: 183,545 sq mi
(475,500 sq km)

Peoples of West Africa

Nigerian

Cameroonian

Africa's greatest-ever migration probably started in what are now eastern Nigeria and Cameroon, about 2,000 years ago. The so-called Bantu peoples spread through much of the continent over many centuries. Their descendants today are speakers of the Niger-Congo family of languages and form the majority in West Africa. Major groups include the Fulani, Wolof, Mende, Bambara, Malinke, Mossi, Yoruba, Ibo, Hausa, Ajan, Ewe, and Tiv. These peoples may share similar ancestry, but they vary greatly in their customs and ways of life. For example, there are about 250 different ethnic groups in Nigeria alone. In addition to local languages, the old colonial languages of English and French are still widely spoken.

Fish, yams, and okra

Nigeria is the most populous country in Africa, and its diet is extremely varied. Small portions of meat are usually served in a hot and spicy sauce. The coasts and many rivers provide shellfish and fish. Yams, cassava, rice, okra, and plantains (cooking bananas) are also popular.

Traders in Togo

On the open patch of ground at the center of many West African towns, as here in Togo, people gather for the district market. Produce and other goods are laid out on the ground for sale, or piled up in enamel bowls or large containers made of hollow gourds called calabashes. Many traders are women, who have few official social rights but considerable economic power.

Benin bronze

Powerful kingdoms, such as Ife, Oyo, and Benin, thrived in the rain forests of what is now southern Nigeria between the 1100s and 1500s. Benin was famous for its craft workers, who carved wood and ivory and cast beautiful figures and heads in brass and

bronze. The Ashanti people of Ghana later became famous for their fine work in gold. Their land was once called the Gold Coast.

Cloth and costume

Men's outfits in northern Nigeria include the *riga*, a long gown worn over trousers, and a small, round hat. Women of this area often wear patterned cotton wraps. Southern Nigerians are often seen in suits, dresses, or jeans and T-shirts.

First foresters

Long before the Bantu peoples moved into the rain forests of West and Central Africa, these lands were home to various short-stature peoples such as the Baka and Kola. Europeans came to name them "Pygmies." Small groups of these ancient peoples still roam the ever-dwindling forests of southern Cameroon. They hunt various animals for meat, gather fruits and other plant foods, and trade them with their Bantu neighbors.

CENTRAL & EAST AFRICA

AFRICA

Central and East Africa takes in huge lakes, forests, savannah, snowy peaks, deserts, and coral islands.

The heart of the African continent is hot and humid. It is dominated by the Congo basin, a vast area of rain forest bordered by volcanoes. This region is rich in minerals and produces cocoa, rubber, and sugarcane. In the late 1800s, the people here experienced great suffering under European rule. Much of the region became independent in the 1960s, but political strife and bloodshed have persisted.

Uganda, Kenya, and Tanzania make up East Africa, with the great lakes of Victoria and Tanganyika. Snowy peaks tower over the savannah. East African farmers herd cattle and grow coffee, cotton, and sisal. Along the shores of the Indian Ocean, coconuts, fish, and spices (especially cloves) are produced. The northeastern peninsula is called the Horn of Africa and is occupied by deserts and the rugged Ethiopian highlands.

On the great river

The Congo River is 2,712 mi (4,374 km) long. It forms a great arc as it flows through the muddy, steamy lands of the rain forest and then rolls on to meet the breakers of the Atlantic Ocean. The river serves as a major highway for villagers, fishers, and traders. It is crowded with riverboats, ferries, water-buses, and wooden dugout canoes.

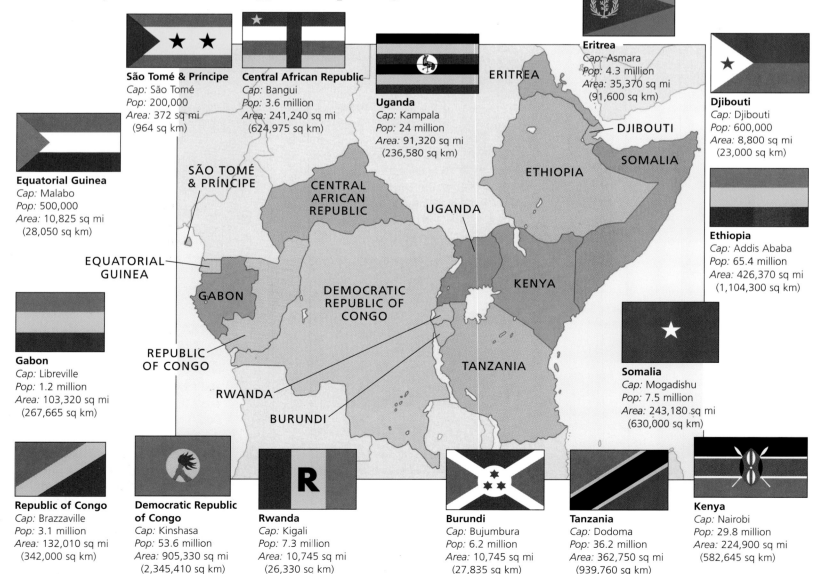

São Tomé & Príncipe
Cap: São Tomé
Pop: 200,000
Area: 372 sq mi
(964 sq km)

Central African Republic
Cap: Bangui
Pop: 3.6 million
Area: 241,240 sq mi
(624,975 sq km)

Uganda
Cap: Kampala
Pop: 24 million
Area: 91,320 sq mi
(236,580 sq km)

Eritrea
Cap: Asmara
Pop: 4.3 million
Area: 35,370 sq mi
(91,600 sq km)

Djibouti
Cap: Djibouti
Pop: 600,000
Area: 8,800 sq mi
(23,000 sq km)

Equatorial Guinea
Cap: Malabo
Pop: 500,000
Area: 10,825 sq mi
(28,050 sq km)

Ethiopia
Cap: Addis Ababa
Pop: 65.4 million
Area: 426,370 sq mi
(1,104,300 sq km)

Gabon
Cap: Libreville
Pop: 1.2 million
Area: 103,320 sq mi
(267,665 sq km)

Somalia
Cap: Mogadishu
Pop: 7.5 million
Area: 243,180 sq mi
(630,000 sq km)

Republic of Congo
Cap: Brazzaville
Pop: 3.1 million
Area: 132,010 sq mi
(342,000 sq km)

Democratic Republic of Congo
Cap: Kinshasa
Pop: 53.6 million
Area: 905,330 sq mi
(2,345,410 sq km)

Rwanda
Cap: Kigali
Pop: 7.3 million
Area: 10,745 sq mi
(26,330 sq km)

Burundi
Cap: Bujumbura
Pop: 6.2 million
Area: 10,745 sq mi
(27,835 sq km)

Tanzania
Cap: Dodoma
Pop: 36.2 million
Area: 362,750 sq mi
(939,760 sq km)

Kenya
Cap: Nairobi
Pop: 29.8 million
Area: 224,900 sq mi
(582,645 sq km)

Map labels: SÃO TOMÉ & PRÍNCIPE, EQUATORIAL GUINEA, GABON, REPUBLIC OF CONGO, RWANDA, BURUNDI, CENTRAL AFRICAN REPUBLIC, DEMOCRATIC REPUBLIC OF CONGO, UGANDA, ERITREA, DJIBOUTI, SOMALIA, ETHIOPIA, KENYA, TANZANIA

Peoples of Central and East Africa

Somali

Tanzanian

There are hundreds of different peoples, languages, and cultures within the regions of Central and East Africa. Most people are speakers of Niger-Congo or Bantu languages. Major groups include the Fang, Kongo, Luba, and Azande of Central Africa and the Ganda, Kikuyu, and Makande of East Africa. The Swahili culture of the East African coast belongs to this group, but over centuries it has blended with Arab and Iranian influences. The oldest people of the region are probably the short-statured ("pygmy") groups such as the Mbuti of the Congo forests. Nilotic peoples include the Acholi, Luo, and Masai of East Africa. Cushitic peoples include the Somali and Galla from the Horn of Africa. The Amhara of Ethiopia are descended from several ancient groups, including explorers and invaders from the Middle East.

Traders

Markets and shops in Central and East Africa sell foodstuffs such as bananas and cornflour, which is mixed into a dough-like hot cereal. Long strips of cotton cloth are dyed in many bright colors and sold to wear as wraps by both women and men. Along the East African coast, the wraps are sometimes printed with bold patterns and Swahili proverbs. Market traders also sell modern plastic items such as bowls, brushes, and buckets. Recorded music is popular too. Bands from the Congo Democratic Republic, blending traditional and modern rhythms, have gained an international following.

On safari

The East African savannah has great herds of elephant, zebra, giraffe, and wildebeest. The first European settlers hunted these wild animals during safaris—expeditions through the wild bush country. Today's safaris are organized not for hunters but for tourists, who marvel at the gazelles and big cats of the Ngorongoro Crater or the Serengeti Plain. Modern developments are harming the habitats of many wild animals, and securing their future is very difficult. Some natural areas are protected within national parks, but the local people also have urgent needs.

People of the forest

The Mbuti people live in the dense, gloomy Ituri forest of the Congo basin. They are a short but nimble people and are experts at rain forest survival. They hunt in roving bands, sheltering in small dome-shaped huts made of branches and leaves. They kill wild animals with bows and arrows, and gather forest fruits, roots, honey, and termites. These foods may be eaten or exchanged with local villagers for farm produce, tools, and other items. The traditional Mbuti way of life is under threat as the forest is infiltrated by loggers, soldiers, tourists, and road builders.

The Masai

The Masai are the main cattle herders of East Africa. Their homeland stretches from the Great Rift Valley, across the plains and savannah of southern Kenya and northern Tanzania. The Masai are a tall people, whose young men wear scarlet or checkered cloaks and carry spears. The women favor broad bead necklaces and earrings. The Masai warriors were much feared by early European explorers in the 1800s. Today, the Masai are fiercely proud of their traditions. Many resent the fact that so much of their land has been taken to create national parks and game reserves for tourists with their cameras.

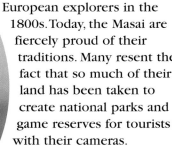

SOUTHERN AFRICA

AFRICA

Africa reaches its southernmost point at Cape Agulhas, in South Africa. The continent is flanked by various islands in the Indian Ocean.

To the south of the Central African forests and the lush highlands of Malawi lie vast areas of bush, scrub, and savannah. Desert borders the foggy Atlantic coast of Namibia, and rivers run dry as they soak into the parched sand of the Kalahari Desert. Cattle are ranched in Botswana. Much of the wealth lies underground, in the form of minerals—South Africa has the world's most productive gold mines. South Africa also has high grasslands known as veld, mountain chains, and farmed land. Crops such as tobacco, beans, and corn are grown in the eastern regions of Southern Africa. However, droughts, floods, and political problems have harmed the economy in parts of the region.

Mauritius

Mauritius is a mountainous, tropical island in the Indian Ocean. Its chief crop is sugar. The island has an exciting history and in the 1600s it was a base for pirates. Its people today are from Africa, Madagascar (named Malagasy), India, China, and France. Its best known animal, sadly long gone, is the dodo.

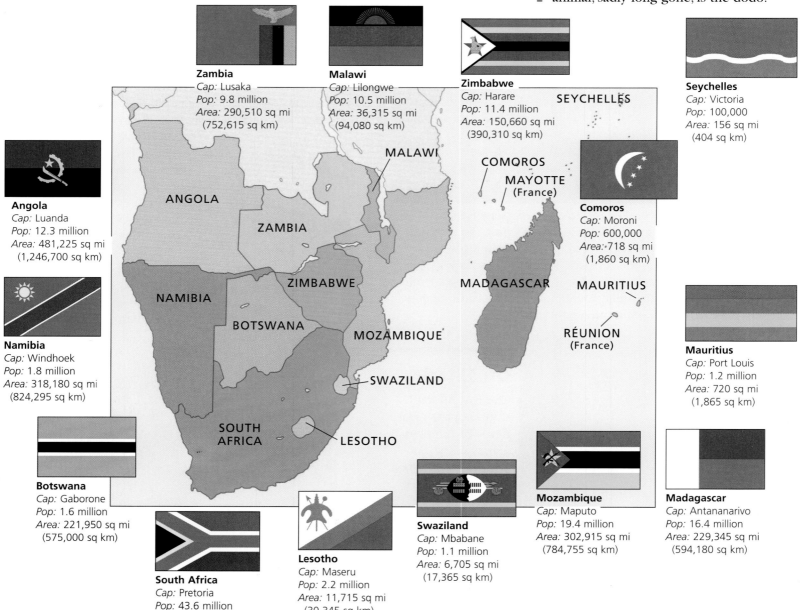

Zambia
Cap: Lusaka
Pop: 9.8 million
Area: 290,510 sq mi
(752,615 sq km)

Malawi
Cap: Lilongwe
Pop: 10.5 million
Area: 36,315 sq mi
(94,080 sq km)

Zimbabwe
Cap: Harare
Pop: 11.4 million
Area: 150,660 sq mi
(390,310 sq km)

Seychelles
Cap: Victoria
Pop: 100,000
Area: 156 sq mi
(404 sq km)

Angola
Cap: Luanda
Pop: 12.3 million
Area: 481,225 sq mi
(1,246,700 sq km)

Comoros
Cap: Moroni
Pop: 600,000
Area: 718 sq mi
(1,860 sq km)

Namibia
Cap: Windhoek
Pop: 1.8 million
Area: 318,180 sq mi
(824,295 sq km)

Mauritius
Cap: Port Louis
Pop: 1.2 million
Area: 720 sq mi
(1,865 sq km)

Botswana
Cap: Gaborone
Pop: 1.6 million
Area: 221,950 sq mi
(575,000 sq km)

Mozambique
Cap: Maputo
Pop: 19.4 million
Area: 302,915 sq mi
(784,755 sq km)

Madagascar
Cap: Antananarivo
Pop: 16.4 million
Area: 229,345 sq mi
(594,180 sq km)

Swaziland
Cap: Mbabane
Pop: 1.1 million
Area: 6,705 sq mi
(17,365 sq km)

Lesotho
Cap: Maseru
Pop: 2.2 million
Area: 11,715 sq mi
(30,345 sq km)

South Africa
Cap: Pretoria
Pop: 43.6 million
Area: 471,369 sq mi
(1,220,845 sq km)

Map labels: ANGOLA, ZAMBIA, MALAWI, ZIMBABWE, NAMIBIA, BOTSWANA, MOZAMBIQUE, SWAZILAND, SOUTH AFRICA, LESOTHO, MADAGASCAR, SEYCHELLES, COMOROS, MAYOTTE (France), MAURITIUS, RÉUNION (France)

Peoples of Southern Africa

Malagasy

Zulu

The Khoi-Koi and San are the main indigenous peoples of Southern Africa. The Khoi-San languages they speak are known for their clicking sounds and guttural utterances. The majority of peoples in the region belong to the Bantu or Niger-Congo group. These include Kongo, Ovimbundu, Xhosa, Zulu, Sotho, Swazi, Ndebele, and many others. South Africa became home to people of Asian and European descent during the period of colonization, after about 1650. They include Afrikaners (Dutch) and English. It was not until 1994 that the white minority in South Africa, who had ruled by state terror under the racist apartheid system, allowed democratic elections for people of all origins. The Malagasy of Madagascar are of mixed Malay-Polynesian and Niger-Congo descent. They form some 18 ethnic groups, of which the largest is the Merina.

Power of the Zambezi

The longest river in Southern Africa is the Zambezi, 1,656 mi (2,650 km) long. It rises near the Angolan border and flows southeast to the Mozambique Channel. On the Zambia-Zimbabwe border, the river tumbles over the Victoria Falls in

a roaring mass of foam. A huge dam downstream, across the river at Kariba, has created the artificial Kariba Lake. The pent-up power of the water drives whirling turbine blades, which generate huge quantities of hydroelectric power, and the lake can be used as a year-round source for irrigation.

The game

A board game known as mancala is played in many parts of Africa—south, north, east, and west. It has various regional names, such as bao or wari. Its origins may have been in Egypt and it was also taken to the Americas long ago by West African slaves. The game can be played on beautiful boards of carved wood, or in simple hollows scraped in the dust, with seeds or beans instead of counters. Other entertainments and sports include soccer, with African teams improving rapidly, and world-class rugby in South Africa.

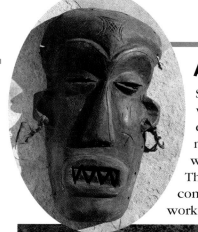

African heritage

Southern Africa has a rich and varied artistic heritage, which is expressed in many ways. Peoples of northern Angola carved impressive wooden masks for their ceremonies. The Sotho national costume includes conical hats made from reed basket work, while Ndebele women wear

intricately woven beads and copper necklaces. Several South African peoples paint their houses with bold and colorful geometric designs. The musical heritage of South Africa, especially its singing, is known worldwide.

Sweet fruit

South Africa's Cape Province has a warm yet mild climate, rather like the Mediterranean lands at the other end of the continent. Fruits grown here include oranges, apples, and grapes for both wine-making and eating. South African wines win many awards.

Cape Town

Cape Town, at the foot of Table Mountain, was founded by the Dutch in 1652. It was a seaport where sailing ships could take on supplies before rounding the continent's southern end at the nearby Cape of Good Hope and Cape Agulhas just to the east. Cape Town is where South Africa, a land of many peoples and races, makes its laws.

OCEANIA

Two continents dominate the windy southern seas. Antarctica is a land mass with such a cold climate that humans have never settled there permanently. The other continent is now known as Oceania. It includes the huge land mass of Australia, too big to be called an island. Also included are the large islands of New Guinea and New Zealand and the countless small islands which are scattered across the South Pacific Ocean.

The first Australians were Aborigines, who probably came from Southeast Asia and began settlement about 50,000 years ago. European ships sailed around Australian coasts in the 1600s and British settlements began in 1788. Much of Australia's interior is made up of desert and dry scrub, so almost all major cities have grown up around the coasts.

Pacific islanders such as Melanesians, Micronesians, and Polynesians also originated in Southeast Asia, migrating across the ocean in canoes between about 3,500 and 1,200 years ago. By 1840, New Zealand was part of the British Empire and the whole Pacific region was soon dominated by European powers. After the 1970s, many Pacific islands became independent nations.

The shearing shed

The Europeans who settled in Australia and New Zealand in the 1800s brought various farm animals with them. Of these, sheep were most suited to the temperate grasslands in New Zealand's South Island and in Australia's southeast states of New South Wales and Victoria. Today's farms, called stations, cover vast areas of countryside. Wool and lamb remain important exports.

Wairakei

The lands all around the Pacific Ocean, known as the Pacific Rim, are in a volcanic danger zone. New Zealanders harness the same underground energy that creates the volcanic eruptions and their associated earthquakes to generate electrical power. At Wairakei, underground water that has turned to steam, deep in the Earth, forces its way to the surface. It is used to drive the turbines that make electricity.

New wines

Australia has many vineyards in Queensland, New South Wales, Victoria, and Western Australia. The most famous vines are tended on the sunny hillsides of South Australia's Barossa Valley, near Adelaide. In recent years, Australian wines have become popular around the world, rivaling the quality of European and American types.

Sydney

The largest city in Oceania is Sydney, capital of Australia's southeast state of New South Wales. It has a population of more than 3.6 million and is located on the beautiful Sydney Harbor. The roofs of its famous waterside opera house are designed to look like sails or shells, and many of the suburbs have beaches. Sydney is a lively center of the arts, industry, commerce, and communications.

Miles
0 — 1,000
Kilometers
0 — 1,600

INDIAN
OCEAN

Timor
Sea

Arafura Sea   Torres Strait

Bismarck Sea

Central Range   PAPUA   New Britain   Bougainville   SOLOMON
NEW GUINEA   Choiseul   ISLANDS
New Ireland
New
Georgia
Guadalcanal
San
Cristobal   Santa
Isabel
Malaita
Banks
Islands

Cape
York

Coral
Sea

Espiritu
Santo

VANUATU

New
Caledonia (Fr.)

PACIFIC
OCEAN

Vanua Levu
FIJI
Viti Levu

TONGA

Norfolk
Island

Lord Howe
Island

North
Cape
North
Island
East
Cape

NEW
ZEALAND
South
Island

Southern Alps

Arnhem
Land   Gulf of
Carpentaria

Kimberley
Plateau   Northern
Fitzroy R.
Territory   Queensland

Great Sandy Desert

AUSTRALIA

Gibson Desert   Macdonnell
Ranges   Simpson
Desert

Western

Australia   L. Eyre

Great Victoria
Desert   South

Australia

Great Australian
Bight

Kangaroo
Island

Darling R.   New

South

Wales

Murray R.   Australian Alps

Victoria

Bass Strait

Tasman
Sea

Tasmania

Great Barrier Reef

Great Dividing Range

Fraser
Island

The Fijians

Fiji is a group of more than 250 islands, the largest being Viti Levu and Vanua Levu. The native peoples have a mixed Melanesian and Polynesian ancestry, and have recorded their traditions in wooden statues and other carvings. Fiji also has a large Indian population, descended from laborers brought to the islands during the British rule of 1874–1970. Fijians catch fish and grow coconuts, sugarcane, and rice. Sugar makes up one-third of Fijian exports. The country also has reserves of gold.

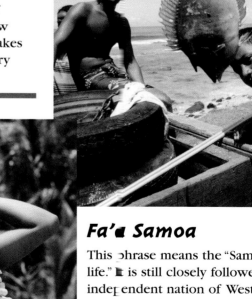

Fa'a Samoa

This phrase means the "Samoan way of life." It is still closely followed in the independent nation of Western Samoa and in American Samoa, a dependency of the U.S. The Samoans are a Polynesian people who live in large family-based groups headed by a chief. Many make their living by fishing, others by farming and forestry. Many Samoans earn their livelihoods in the U.S. and New Zealand.

83

OCEANIA

Australia, Papua New Guinea, and New Zealand are by far the largest Oceanic nations. Fewer than 3 million people live on all other islands.

Australia is the giant of the southern oceans, but its harsh interior, or outback, is sparsely populated. Most people live in the big coastal cities such as Brisbane, Sydney, Melbourne, Adelaide, and Perth. Australia has one of the most important economies of the Pacific Rim (others being Korea, Japan, Canada, and the western U.S.). Its major industries include chemicals, timber, paper, and tourism. Papua New Guinea is much less industrial—a land of wooded mountains, lowland rain forests, plains, and islands. Resources include gold, copper, coffee, rubber, timber, and fish. New Zealand has fertile lands, orchards, and pastures below the high peaks of the Southern Alps. Industry is based in the larger cities of Auckland, Wellington, Christchurch, and Dunedin.

Broken Hill

A giant mining truck carries metal-rich ores at Broken Hill, in the Australian state of New South Wales. Australia is one of the top world producers of iron, nickel, and zinc and also mines coal, gold, uranium, copper, and precious stones like opals. Miners lead a tough life, often in remote outback towns.

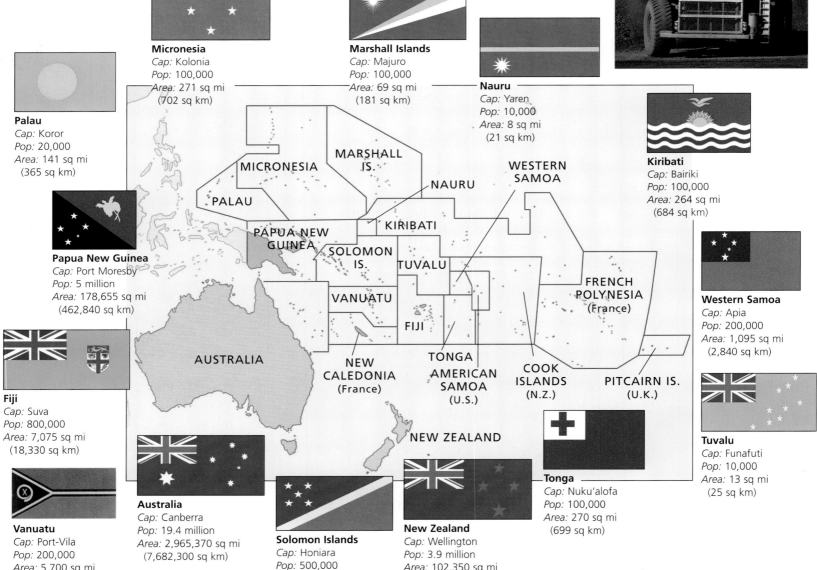

Micronesia
Cap: Kolonia
Pop: 100,000
Area: 271 sq mi
(702 sq km)

Marshall Islands
Cap: Majuro
Pop: 100,000
Area: 69 sq mi
(181 sq km)

Nauru
Cap: Yaren
Pop: 10,000
Area: 8 sq mi
(21 sq km)

Palau
Cap: Koror
Pop: 20,000
Area: 141 sq mi
(365 sq km)

Kiribati
Cap: Bairiki
Pop: 100,000
Area: 264 sq mi
(684 sq km)

Papua New Guinea
Cap: Port Moresby
Pop: 5 million
Area: 178,655 sq mi
(462,840 sq km)

Western Samoa
Cap: Apia
Pop: 200,000
Area: 1,095 sq mi
(2,840 sq km)

Fiji
Cap: Suva
Pop: 800,000
Area: 7,075 sq mi
(18,330 sq km)

Tuvalu
Cap: Funafuti
Pop: 10,000
Area: 13 sq mi
(25 sq km)

Vanuatu
Cap: Port-Vila
Pop: 200,000
Area: 5,700 sq mi
(14,765 sq km)

Australia
Cap: Canberra
Pop: 19.4 million
Area: 2,965,370 sq mi
(7,682,300 sq km)

Solomon Islands
Cap: Honiara
Pop: 500,000
Area: 11,500 sq mi
(29,790 sq km)

New Zealand
Cap: Wellington
Pop: 3.9 million
Area: 102,350 sq mi
(265,150 sq km)

Tonga
Cap: Nuku'alofa
Pop: 100,000
Area: 270 sq mi
(699 sq km)

Map labels: MARSHALL IS., MICRONESIA, WESTERN SAMOA, NAURU, PALAU, KIRIBATI, PAPUA NEW GUINEA, SOLOMON IS., TUVALU, FRENCH POLYNESIA (France), VANUATU, FIJI, AUSTRALIA, NEW CALEDONIA (France), TONGA, AMERICAN SAMOA (U.S.), COOK ISLANDS (N.Z.), PITCAIRN IS. (U.K.), NEW ZEALAND

Peoples of Australia and the Pacific

Aboriginal

Fijian

As the natives of Australia, Aboriginals now form a minority. They only gained full civil rights in 1967. The peoples of New Guinea form many different ethnic groups within the Indo-Pacific family, such as the Huli, Melpa, and Sepik. Melanesians live on the Trobriand and Solomon Islands and on Fiji. The Micronesians live in Micronesia and the Marshall Islands. Polynesians, including the Maoris (the first New Zealanders), are spread across a wide area, from New Zealand to Samoa. People of European descent in Australia and New Zealand include the English, Welsh, Scots, Irish, Greeks, Italians, Dutch, Scandinavians, Germans, and Poles. English is the common language. French are found in New Caledonia and French Polynesia. Asian communities include Lebanese, Chinese, Indians, Thai, and Vietnamese in Australia, and Indians in Fiji.

The Maori

New Zealand's indigenous people are called the Maoris. They have a Polynesian culture which has remained a source of pride long after the arrival of Europeans and city-based ways of life. This is expressed in powerful dances such as the *hakka*. Maoris have a long tradition of woodcarving. Ornately carved timber roofs and doorposts adorn many typical Maori meeting houses, or *wharerunanga*. Nine percent of New Zealanders have Maori ancestry. Other Polynesian groups make up three percent.

Pacific life

Missionaries from Europe brought Christianity and western dress to the islands of the South Pacific in the 1800s. But ancient traditions are still reflected in the social organization, in travel by canoe, and by a great love of singing, dancing, and feasting. Most islanders survive by fishing and farming, or work in the tourist business, welcoming visitors especially from Asia and the Americas. Some islands, such as phosphate-rich Nauru, have been devastated by mining operations.

Sports mad

Australians and New Zealanders are great lovers of outdoor life, barbecue cooking, country treks, and team sports. They both have world-class rugby and cricket teams, and Australia has also developed its own sport—Australian rules football. Swimming, surfing, yachting, and tennis are also popular. International rugby teams are fielded by Fiji and Samoa, too.

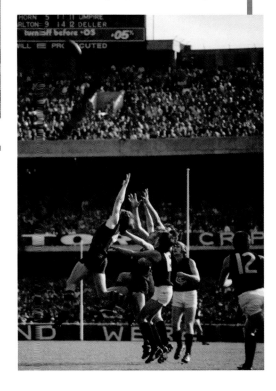

Island crops

Taro, a starchy root crop, is grown on many South Pacific islands. Sweet potatoes, cassava, yams, breadfruit, and bananas are other important sources of food. Most of these are grown for the family and village, since self-sufficiency is important in such remote lands. Coconuts are an important industry, with exports of the dried flesh, named copra.

GLOSSARY

capital The chief city in a country, which is normally the center of government. It is not always the biggest city.

cash crop A crop which is grown not for local eating or use, but for sale or export.

citizen (1) A person considered as a member of society. (2) The member of a particular nation. For example: "She is a Canadian citizen."

citrus fruit Oranges or any similar fruits, such as lemons, grapefruit, limes, or tangerines, grown in warm countries.

civilization A society which has made progress in political organization, law, arts, and crafts.

climate The pattern of weather recorded in one place or region over a long period.

colonize (1) To make a settlement in a foreign land. (2) To take over the land or even the government of a foreign place.

communist Believing in public, shared ownership of industry and land, and in government by the working people.

continent One of the major geographical divisions of the world's land masses, such as Asia, Africa, or North America.

culture (1) The way in which a group of people live, including social organization, customs, language, and religion. (2) Forms of expression such as arts, music, drama, dance, or writing.

delta (1) The splitting of a river into separate channels as it nears the coast. (2) The region surrounding these waterways.

democracy Government by an elected assembly, such as a parliament, rather than by one (king or a dictator) or a few people.

dependency A land which is ruled by another nation, such as a colony.

drought A long period without rainfall or other forms of moisture.

economy The way in which money, work, or employment is organized.

empire A group of different countries or territories which all come under the rule of a single government or an emperor.

environment The natural world in which we live, its soils, rocks, plants, and animals.

erode To wear away. Rocks are eroded by waves, rain, and wind.

ethnic group A group of people sharing common descent, customs, or language.

export (1) To send or sell abroad. (2) An item being exported.

famine A period of lack of food when many people go hungry.

federation Many regions united together, such as the United States of America.

government The national or regional body which organizes society by making and enforcing laws.

heavy industry An industry such as steel-making, shipbuilding, mining, or the manufacture of heavy machinery.

homeland The area in which a particular people live, either within a nation or across national frontiers. For example, Lapland, the homeland of the Saami people, is in Norway, Sweden, Finland, and Russia.

humid Moist, containing water vapor.

hurricane A whirling, violent, tropical storm of the West Atlantic Ocean. Tropical storms in the Indian Ocean are called cyclones, whereas in the Pacific they are called typhoons.

hydroelectric power Electricity which has been made or generated by water-driven turbines, usually at a dam.

independent Recognized as free and self-governing, and not controlled by others.

indigenous Originating in a place, rather than arriving later. Native Americans and Australian Aborigines are examples of indigenous peoples.

irrigation Bringing water to an area so that crops can be grown, often by building channels or aqueducts or pipelines.

isthmus A narrow strip joining two larger areas of land. One example is the Isthmus of Panama, in Central America.

land mass A large geographical division of land on Earth. For example, two joined continents, Europe and Asia, make up the Eurasian land mass.

mineral Any substance which can be extracted from the Earth's crust (rocks), usually by mining or drilling, such as metal ores, diamonds, or oil.

monarchy Rule by a king or queen.

monsoon A seasonal wind of the Indian Ocean, which brings heavy rainfall to southern Asia.

native Originating in a place, rather than arriving later. For example, the breadfruit is a native plant of the South Pacific islands.

nutrition Providing someone with the kind of food they need to stay healthy and strong.

ore Mined rock, from which metals or similar substances are extracted.

paddy field A field which is flooded so that rice seedlings can be grown. "Paddy" is the name given to raw, husky grains of rice before they are cleaned and treated.

pampas The grasslands of Argentina, in South America, used for ranching cattle.

parliament An assembly elected by citizens to govern a country, known in some places by other names, like senate.

peninsula A piece of land which is almost surrounded by water, such as a headland.

plateau An area of flat land usually at a high altitude above sea level.

polder Land that has been reclaimed from the sea, especially in the Netherlands.

politics The government of nations or methods of bringing about social change.

pollution The poisoning or damage of land, sea, or air, for example, by factory waste or exhaust fumes.

population The number of people living in any one place.

prairie The grasslands of North America, used for growing crops and raising cattle.

rain forest Lush, thick forest in lands with a heavy rainfall.

refugee Somebody who flees to another country in order to escape hardship or persecution at home.

republic A country that has no king or queen. It is normally governed by elected representatives and headed by a president.

resource Useful or valuable materials to be found in a country or region, such as timber, iron ore, coal, or oil.

salt lake A lake in a desert region, full of mineral salts. As the water turns to vapor in the hot sun, salt is left behind.

savannah African grasslands, dotted with trees and thickets.

service industry An industry which makes its money by offering services to the public, such as catering or banking.

steppes The grasslands of Eurasia, used for growing crops or grazing animals.

subsistence farming Growing just enough crops for the needs of one's own family or community.

suburbs Outlying districts of a large town or city, away from the center.

temperate Moderate, mild.

terraces Flat strips or fields cut into the slope of a hillside, which make it easier to grow and irrigate crops and retain the soil.

terrain The lie of the land or type of landscape—rocky, for example, or sandy.

territory An area of land within a country, claimed by a country or colonized.

textile Any cloth produced by weaving.

tributary A river that joins a larger one.

tropical Belonging to the lands which lie just to the north and south of the Equator, where it is usually warm all year.

tundra Treeless landscapes, as found in the Arctic, covered by ice and snow in the winter. The surface melts briefly during the summer, but the lower soil remains deep-frozen all year round.

turbine A machine with spinning fan-shaped blades called vanes, used for generating electricity. It may be powered by water, steam, or wind.

vegetation The types of plants which grow in a particular region of the world.

INDEX

Abbreviations: t-top, m-middle, b-bottom, r-right, l-left, c-center
Indexer: Jane Parker **Artwork credits:** 46br—Carol Daniel. All maps—Stephen Sweet.

Photograph credits:
Abbreviations: t-top, m-middle, b-bottom, r-right, l-left, c-center
7tl, 7br, 7mr, 41bl—Helen Parker.fc tl, fc br, bc all, 5bl, 7ml, 9bl, 12tr, 15tr, 17tr, 20tr, 21mrt, 21bl, 22r, 24tr, 32c, 32ml, 33ml, 35ml, 35bl, 36ml both, 37mrt, 38tr, 38c, 39mt, 39tr, 39ml, 39c, 41tr, 41ml, 41mr, 41mbr, 42mr, 43ml, 43mb, 44bl, 45mr both, 46mr, 47mrt, 47mrb, 49ml both, 49bl, 52tl, 52tr, 53tr, 54tr, 56tr, 57tr, 64ml, 67mrb, 67bm, 80tr—Digital Stock. fc mr, fc bl, 4bl, 7tr, 7c, 8bl, 11bl, 12mr, 14ml, 17br, 19mt, 21ml, 21mrb, 35bm, 43mrt, 44c, 45mt, 45ml, 45br 47ml, 51mr, 54bl, 72ml, 72c, 72trt, 75tl, 75ml, 75c both, 75bl, 77mrt, 79bl, 79br, 81c both, 81bm, 82t, 82mr both, 82bm both, 84 both, 85tl, 85br—Corbis. 1, 41mt, 47mt, 62bl, 65mrb, 65tr, 67tl, 67c, 67mrt, 67bl, 68ml, 69bl, 71mlt, 71mlb, 71mrb, 71br both—Flat Earth. 2-3, 68mr, 69br—PhotoEssentials. 4c, 11br, 12c, 12bl, 13bl, 14tr, 15mt, 15ml, 15c, 16br, 17tr, 18tr both, 19tr, 19mlb, 19bl, 21tl, 23tr, 23ml, 23bl, 23br, 24ct, 25br, 27mr, 28bl, 29mt, 29tr, 29ml, 32tr, 36bl, 36mb, 36c, 37tl, 37mt, 37ml, 37br both, 40mlt, 40mr, 42ml, 43mt, 43mrb, 45tr, 45bl, 46ml, 47tl, 47tr, 47bl, 49mr, 49mt, 50bl, 50br, 51tl, 51mt, 52c, 53tl, 53mt, 53trl, 53ml, 53br both 54m both, 54br, 55bl, 57mt, 57ml, 59tl, 59mt, 59tr both, 59br, 60tr, both, 61tl, 61mt, 61tr both, 61mr, 62mr, 63 all, 64br, 64c, 65mt, 65mrt, 65ml, 65b both, 66tr, 67mt, 68t, 69mt, 69tr both, 69mr, 69c both, 70 all, 71tl, 71mt, 72b, 72trb, 73mlt, 73br, 74tr, 75tr, 75br, 79tr, 79c, 81tr both, 81bl, 83 all, 85mt, 85tr both, 85cb—Corel. 4br, 19mr—John Deere. 6b—Anthony Bannister; Gallo Images/CORBIS. 7tl, 7mr, 7br, 41mb—Helen Parker. 7bm—O. Alamany & E. Vicens/CORBIS. 8tr, 8mr, 17mrb, 20c, 37c, 40mlb, 42tr, 44tr, 45tl, 45mb, 46bl, 71tr both, 72mr, 77tr—Select Pictures. 9tm—Scania. 8ml—Gail Mooney/CORBIS. 9br, 10br—Sergio Dorantes/CORBIS. 10bl—David H. Wells/CORBIS. 13b, 57tl, 75mt—Paul A. Souders/CORBIS. 15tl, 17tl, 17mt, 19tl, 21mt, 23tl, 23mt, 27tl, 29tl, 31tl, 31mt, 39tl, 43tl, 65tl, 69tl, 79mr, 81tl—Hollingsworth Studios Inc. 15mr—James Marshall/CORBIS. 16tr both, 16mr, 17mrt, 17bl, 18ml, 20br both, 21tr—Photodisc. 18c, 51ml, 60ml, 82ml, 85ct—Dave G. Houser/CORBIS. 19mlt—Jerry Cooke/CORBIS. 24bl, 25ml, 25bl, 29br, 31mr—Argentinian Embassy, London. 24cb—Marc Garanger/CORBIS. 26m, 79mt—Wolfgang Kaehler/CORBIS. 26ml, 27mt, 27ml, 27bm—Colombian Embassy, London. 27tr—Craig Lovell/CORBIS. 28br—Neil Rabinowitz/CORBIS. 29mb—Stephanie Maze/CORBIS. 30tr, 51bl, 77ml, 78tr—Paul Almasy/CORBIS. 31ml—Pablo Corral V/CORBIS. 31br, 40bm—Galen Rowell/CORBIS. 32br, 58mt—NASA. 33bl, 37tr, 57c—Stockbyte. 33br—French Embassy, London. 34tr, 35mt, 35mr—Finnish Embassy, London. 35tl—Buddy Mays/CORBIS. 35tr—Adam Woolfit/CORBIS. 38bl—Dave Bartruff/CORBIS. 39bl—Sally A. Morgan; Ecoscene/CORBIS. 41tl—Catherine Karnow/CORBIS. 47c—Austrian Embassy, London. 49tl, 49tr—Slovenian Embassy, London. 48mr—Michael Freeman/CORBIS. 48br, 73mlb—Peter Turnley/CORBIS. 49br—Barry Lewis/CORBIS. 51tr both—Estonian Embassy, London. 51bmt—Hans Georg Roth/CORBIS. 51bmb—Roman Soumar/CORBIS. 53mr—Robbie Jacks/CORBIS. 53bl—Bernard and Catherine Desjeux/CORBIS. 55br—Colin Garratt; Milepost 92.5/CORBIS. 55bm—Bennett Dean; Eye Ubiquitous/CORBIS. 56bl—Roger Wood/CORBIS. 57mr—Annie Griffiths Belt/CORBIS. 57br—Carmen Redondo/CORBIS. 57bm — Steve Raymer/CORBIS. 58tr—Vince Streano/CORBIS. 59ml, 76tr—Charles and Josette Lenars/CORBIS. 59c—Jon Spaull/CORBIS. 59mrt—Ric Ergenbright/CORBIS. 59bl—David Samuel Robbins/CORBIS. 59bm—Caroline Penn/CORBIS. 61ml—Nik Wheeler/CORBIS. 61bm—Earl & Nazima Kowall/CORBIS. 62tr—Jonathon Blair/CORBIS. 67ml—Michael S. Yamashita/CORBIS. 75mr—Tiziana and Gianni Baldizzone/CORBIS. 77mt—Otto Lang/CORBIS. 77tl, 77bm, 85bl—Owen Franken/CORBIS. 77bl—Christie's Images/CORBIS. 77mrb—Tony Wilson-Bligh; Papilio/CORBIS. 79tl—David Turnley/CORBIS. 81mt—Roger De La Harpe; Gallo Images/CORBIS. 81ml—Robert van der Hilst/CORBIS.